THE MEDIEVAL FEATHERS

TAROT

Artwork & Concept by Alejandro R. Rozán

Text by Jay R. Rivera

THE MEDIEVAL FEATHERS
TAROT

Artwork & Concept © 2024 Alejandro R. Rozán
Text © 2024 Jay R. Rivera

All rights reserved. Other than for personal use, no part of these cards or this book may be reproduced in any way, in whole or in part, without the written consent of the copyright holder or publisher. This publication is intended for spiritual and emotional guidance only. The content is not intended to replace medical assistance or treatment. The views and opinions expressed by the author, both within and outside of this publication, do not necessarily reflect the views of the publisher.

Published by Blue Angel Publishing®
80 Glen Tower Drive, Glen Waverley,
Victoria, Australia 3150

info@blueangelonline.com
www.blueangelonline.com

Edited by Peter Loupelis
Designed by Sunshine Connelly

Blue Angel is a registered trademark
of Blue Angel Gallery Pty Ltd

ISBN: 978-1-922573-89-6

CONTENTS

Author's Acknowledgment — 9
Illustrator's Acknowledgment — 9

Messages from Heaven — 11
Interpretive Techniques — 21
Card Spreads — 30

Card Meanings — 37

About the Artist — 219
About the Author — 220

MAJOR ARCANA

0. The Fool - 38

1. The Magician - 40

2. The Popess - 42

3. The Empress - 45

4. The Emperor - 47

5. The Pope - 49

6. The Lovers - 51

7. The Chariot - 53

8. Justice - 55

9. The Hermit - 57

10. The Wheel of Fortune - 59

11. Strength - 61

12. The Hanged Man - 63

13. Death - 66

14. Temperance - 68

15. The Devil - 71

16. Lightning - 73

16. The House of God - 75

17. The Star - 77

18. The Moon - 79

19. The Sun - 81

20. Judgment - 83

21. The World - 85

22. The Querent - 87

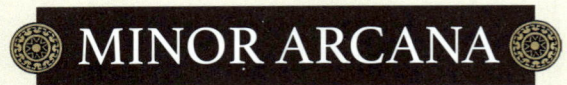

MINOR ARCANA

LES DENIERS
COINS

Ace of Coins - 91

Two of Coins - 93

Three of Coins - 95

Four of Coins - 97

Five of Coins - 99

Six of Coins - 101

Seven of Coins - 103

Eight of Coins - 105

Nine of Coins - 107

Ten of Coins - 109

Page of Coins - 111

Knight of Coins - 113

Queen of Coins - 115

King of Coins - 117

LES COUPES
CUPS

Ace of Cups - 120

Two of Cups - 123

Three of Cups - 125

Four of Cups - 127

Five of Cups - 129

Six of Cups - 131

Seven of Cups - 133

Eight of Cups - 135

Nine of Cups - 137

Ten of Cups - 139

Page of Cups - 141

Knight of Cups - 144

Queen of Cups - 147

King of Cups - 150

LES BASTONS
WANDS

Ace of Wands - 154

Two of Wands - 156

Three of Wands - 158

Four of Wands - 160

Five of Wands - 162

Six of Wands - 164

Seven of Wands - 166

Eight of Wands - 168

Nine of Wands - 170

Ten of Wands - 172

Page of Wands - 174

Knight of Wands - 176

Queen of Wands - 179

King of Wands - 182

LES ÉPÉES
SWORDS

Ace of Swords - 186

Two of Swords - 189

Three of Swords - 191

Four of Swords - 193

Five of Swords - 195

Six of Swords - 197

Seven of Swords - 199

Eight of Swords - 201

Nine of Swords - 203

Ten of Swords - 205

Page of Swords - 207

Knight of Swords - 209

Queen of Swords - 212

King of Swords - 215

Author's Acknowledgment

To my parents, María and José, and siblings Jessica, Joanna, and Jaime, and to my niece, Aleyna — your constant support and encouragement make everything I do fulfilling. To my fur babies Candy, Molly, and Lucky — you are my light and the source of my inspiration, which never fails. To my grandfather, Fernando Rivera, for passing down your imagination and gift of writing.

To all the birds who bestow us with their feathers as a message that we must heed to understand.

To Peter Loupelis, a fantastic and gifted editor whose encouragement never fails. To Blue Angel Publishing and staff, thank you for believing in this project and for working on it with me.

—Jay R. Rivera

Illustrator's Acknowledgment

To all the women in my family: My mother Mileide, my aunt Guelsy and my cousin Claudia, thank you for supporting me in everything that I do. And to my grandmother Eulalia who planted the seed of art I inherited.

—Alejandro R. Rozán

MESSAGES FROM HEAVEN

Imagine you have a dream, and you see a piece of medieval art in that dream. It's broken up into 80 pieces and scattered across the dry landscape. You look up and see a flock of every imaginable bird above you. As they soar across the sky, their feathers—the essence of their being—fall onto the pieces of the artwork before you. They intertwine and become one, providing you with visions of the past and future.

History is a gateway into the past, allowing us to learn from our mistakes and avoid repeating them. On the other hand, feathers are messages from Heaven to inform us of what the future holds.

Images of the Medieval Era depict life as risky and challenging. Difficult conditions were commonly experienced, and all forms of suffering and cruelty were the norm. If you lived in these times, you might have found yourself placing your trust in people—such as those in positions of authority—who turned out to be disrespectful and untrustworthy. When you needed them the most, those who professed to care and had the means to assist were found wanting. The Medieval Era is a metaphor for our day-to-day struggles.

When our happiness is diminished, and we frequently feel threatened and insecure, we are blind to our potential to achieve. On the brink of despair, messages of hope arrive from the heavens, elevating and guiding us to seek paths toward a greater future. The feathers—messages from Heaven—inspire and empower us to take action and start something new. They provide insight into how we comprehend matters. They reveal our hearts' desires and help us consider our divine purpose.

These messages from Heaven have landed on the cards, and these cards have landed in front of you. Let them take you on a journey of self-discovery.

The meanings of these cards are unique, matching the original illustrations influenced by the earliest decks of the 15th to 17th centuries. This guidebook provides the interpretations of the cards, as well as some background on the tarot, how to use the cards, and some layouts for you to practice your readings. The images on the cards contain layers of meaning for you to discover. Each entry contains a brief description of the card, highlighting any specific features pertaining to the meanings.

For this deck, not only did the images take inspiration from their antique predecessors, but the divinatory meanings did, too. The 'upright' and 'reversed' messages of the cards are inspired by the *Livre de Thot* tarot of 1789. Created by the French occultist Etteilla (Jean-Baptiste

Alliette 1738–1791), it is considered to be the first tarot deck with interpretations of the images explicitly for the use of divinatory readings. In that deck, the 'upright' and 'reversed' meanings were completely different from each other. This device was incorporated into *The Medieval Feathers Tarot* to give it a fresh and different approach for tarot readers.

Finally, there is an interpretation of the unique feature of the feather. The conventional interpretations have been included as the 'feather' section for those who are more accustomed to reading with the traditional meanings.

The court cards are complex. Their meanings are divided into two sections: The first is 'in a situation', indicating actions or circumstances in the querent's life. The second is as an archetypal person, representing personalities or traits of someone described within a reading. Both can be right, and your intuition will guide you to which is relevant to the reading.

The Inspiration

The Medieval Feathers Tarot echoes tarot decks from the past. The images on the cards came from Alejandro's dreams. No matter how hard he tried, he couldn't remember what he dreamed about — only that it involved feathers and medieval themes. When our inspiration to create comes in a dream and we can't remember the details, it never hurts to look back in history to see how we can replace that missing puzzle piece. So, he chose to combine medieval art with bird feathers and draw influence from other vintage tarot cards. The primary goal of developing this tarot deck was to resurrect these historical decks.

Because *The Medieval Feathers Tarot* is a pip deck rather than a scenic deck (such as the *Rider-Waite* and many other modern decks), it includes direct references for the minors and parts of the trumps from the earlier Italian and French tarot decks of the 15th and 18th centuries. Each picture incorporates features from different tarot decks to give it a feeling of individuality, in both the Major and Minor Arcana.

These are the decks which inspired the illustrations within the cards:

> *Tarot de Jean Noblet* (1650)
> *Tarot de Jacques Vieville* (c. 1650)
> *The Cary–Yale Sheet* (15th century)
> *Budapest Tarot* (15th century)
> *Flamand or Vandenborre Tarot* (1780)
> *Tarocco Bolognese* (1442)
> *Medieval Tarocchi* (1500)
> *Pierpont–Morgan Bergamo Tarot* (1452)
> *Visconti di Modrone Tarot* (c. 1450)
> *Minchiate Tarot* (c. 1466)
> *Zodiac Anatomy Homosignorum* (for *XXII Le Consultant*)

Find images from these tarot decks online and compare; you'll see the similarities. It's impossible to replicate the tarot decks listed above, and many have tried to. The essence of those tarot decks is infused in this deck and is now yours to use.

We hope you enjoy using these cards as much as we did creating them!

The Tarot and Its Uses

Tarot cards were initially employed to play games similar to poker. French occultists in the 18th century began to utilize them as a divination tool.

Nowadays, tarot cards are used for divination, predicting scenarios, self-reflection, or finding a solution to a query. There are many ways to interpret tarot cards, and each card has its meaning, which does not necessarily have to be followed.

There is no potential danger to using tarot cards, especially when you want to discover answers for questions, but please keep your intentions clean and pure.

The tarot is a tool like a hammer — you can use it to hurt, or you can use it to build. With the tarot, you can build awareness and healing. But you can also hurt someone (or yourself) by using lies and manipulation or scaring them with daunting predictions. Just remember, what goes around comes around. It comes down to the purpose behind why you are consulting the cards. Always remember to do right by the cards and use them to help people and yourself, not cause pain or suffering.

A tarot deck is traditionally made up of 78 cards and usually comprises two parts. The first, known as the Major Arcana, has 22 cards with images of characters or scenes. Known as 'trumps', they are numbered from 0 to XXI, each with a unique name.

The Minor Arcana is the second portion. It has 56 cards separated into four suits: Coins, Wands, Cups, and Swords. They have a more straightforward design. Each suit has ten 'pip' cards, displaying the number of the symbols described — for example, the Two of Coins displays two coins, while the Ten of Wands displays ten wands, and so on.

This section also has 16 court cards—four per suit—which include the Kings, Queens, Knights, and Pages. They are typically depicted as persons who govern the suit to which they are appointed.

Tarot is a never-ending lesson. As time passes, when working with and studying the tarot, you will always uncover and learn something new that you had no idea existed. The best part is learning about yourself. Of course, if you're new to tarot, you don't want to exhaust yourself. It's okay to take a break to recover and get back to work when you're ready.

The Titles in *The Medieval Feathers Tarot*

If you know French, you'll notice some card titles are misspelled or grammatically wrong. This is not a mistake — there's a purpose for this.

Alejandro wanted the titles and pictures to be as accurate as possible. While the original antique decks were Italian in origin, he chose to follow the structure of the cards produced in Marseilles, France, in the 17th and 18th centuries. *Tarot de Marseilles* is the name given to several decks produced at this time. They were unique in that the pip cards continued the tradition of representing swords, wands, coins, and cups, whereas elsewhere in France these cards were produced showing the symbols of playing cards we are familiar with today — spades, clubs, diamonds, and hearts.

The other unique feature of these decks was that they maintained the four court cards in each suit—King, Queen, Knight, and Page—whereas the French tradition of producing cards only showed three — King, Queen, and Jack. As such, the titles follow those shown on the Marseilles decks, which introduced the *XVI La Maison Dieu* to replace the Italian *XVI La Foudre*.

French—*la langue de l'amour* (the language of love)—is such a beautiful language. Since this tarot deck embodies most of the decks that came before it, we figured the titles in French are a perfect homage to that.

In some of the titles of the cards you will find that certain words are written with a V instead of a U. There is a reason for this. This was how the words were written in Old Latin. Since French is a romance language derived from Latin, it adopted this same practice. That is why the sounds 'u' were written as a 'v' in Old French. This was maintained for the card titles to commemorate the tradition of the historical tarot decks.

The Bonus Cards

Typically, there are 78 cards in a deck, but there is an exception with this deck. There are two additional cards that may be utilized in various ways, depending on your preferences.

The first card is *XXII Le Consultant,* representing the querent for whom the reading is being done or a situation/matter of concern. Some tarot readers have a procedure whereby they remove a card from the deck that represents the nature of the querent or the situation in question. This card is used as a focal point. For example, they may remove the Two of Cups if the question is about love, or the Queen of Pentacles if the reading is for a brunette-haired woman. To avoid removing a card from your reading, *XXII Le Consultant* is a perfect fit to represent people and/or situations. This card does have a divinatory meaning, so you can shuffle it into the deck and include it in your readings.

The second card is *XVI La Maison Dieu,* nowadays known as 'The Tower'. For this deck, and according to its system, *XVI La Foudre* has taken its place. *XVI La Maison Dieu* was created and placed in this deck for those wanting the modern card for their readings. The divinatory meanings of these two cards vary slightly, so you can include one or both in your readings.

We wanted to include these bonus cards as a heartfelt thank you, to you, the owner of this tarot deck.

INTERPRETIVE TECHNIQUES

There are many ways to read tarot cards and build layers of meaning. One does not have to rely entirely on the divinatory interpretations of each card to find the answers they seek. Here are a few techniques to help you read the cards while studying and learning the divinatory meanings of the cards.

Once you have mastered the divinatory meanings and used them with these methods, you will be amazed by how you can create a meaningful narrative as you interpret the cards, not to mention the messages that will proliferate.

Using the Numbers

All tarot decks have numbers linked to the cards. For example, the Major Arcana is traditionally numbered from 0–21. There are four sets of cards numbered from 1 to 10 in the Minor Arcana. When a digit appears repeatedly in a spread, it carries a message that hints at an answer to your reading.

Here is a list of each number and its numerological significance:

1. New beginnings, opportunity, potential
2. Balance, partnership, duality
3. Creativity, groups, growth
4. Structure, stability, manifestation
5. Change, instability, conflict
6. Communication, cooperation, harmony
7. Reflection, assessment, knowledge
8. Mastery, action, accomplishment
9. Fruition, attainment, fulfillment
10. Completion, end of a cycle, renewal

For example, if you draw five cards, and there are three 6s then it may suggest that there needs to be more peaceful communication. If you draw eight cards with four 3s and four 10s, how could you interpret that? You can decide which one you prefer (the 3s or the 10s), depending on the context of the reading. It could also be a combination of both — for example, the completion of a group creative project. Trust your intuition with how you interpret this information.

Using Odds and Evens

What if you were to find patterns of odd or even numbers? For example, a layout of six cards has four even numbers and two are odd, or vice versa. What happens now?

Even numbers indicate balance, good life, and incredible energy around the circumstances you are in. If the quantity of even numbers is more significant, you may be confident that you have nothing to worry about.

When there are too many odd numbers, the energy is uneven, disruptive, and conflicting forces might stymie the answer you seek. This isn't always bad — it merely indicates that additional attention is required.

An equal number of even and odd numbers indicates a healthy balance and that it should remain that way for a time without being disturbed.

The numbers are beneficial, but you don't have to rely entirely on them. Consider them as extra assistance when you need more interpretation, especially if you enjoy dealing with numbers.

Using the Suits

The suits each have their own interpretation. When you obtain multiples of them in your reading, individually or in combination, they may signal what must be addressed and given attention to.

***Les Deniers*/Coins** — the body, everything material and physical, practical, and conservative

***Les Coupes*/Cups** — the emotions, connection, the sentimental and romantic, social, spiritual

***Les Bastons*/Wands** — desire, passionate and outgoing, energetic, creative, conflictive

***Les Épées*/Swords** — the intellect, rationality, the verbal, decisive, aggressive

Using the Court Cards

The court cards can represent a person or a situation, and this is where your intuition has to decide which one is coming through. You can also associate polarity with them — for example, *Le Roy* and *Le Cavalier* are active, while *La Reyne* and *Le Valet* are passive.

Court cards are usually the most difficult to master and interpret, but it can be done with practice and a touch of intuition. Before you know it, they will be speaking volumes.

***Le Valet/* The Page** may represent an individual who is a novice at a trade or field and may have little to no knowledge. On the downside, it can mean someone is immature and irresponsible. When multiple *Valet* cards appear, you have important information needed to think outside the box and to initiate what you want. Just avoid deviating into fantasy land.

***Le Cavalier/* The Knight** may represent an individual working hard and a few steps away from advancing toward a goal they have been working on. Or they may be an aide who is ready to serve. On the downside, it can represent someone who is lazy and not goal-oriented. Many *Cavalier* cards in a single reading signifies that the courage needed to push through is present. It's only a matter of time for you to find the courage you need to help you break through stagnation.

***La Reyne/* The Queen** may represent an individual who does anything they can to receive achievements or conduct realization toward personal matters. When there are many *Reyne* cards in a reading, this usually denotes that you have to get in touch with your softer side in order to see things differently.

***Le Roy/* The King** may represent an individual who regularly acts from a position of power and possesses the ability of control. If there are many *Roy* cards, the energy is dominant and ruling. This being said, there is no way you will be defeated, and your plans will not go astray.

Using the Feathers

While the feathers have a specific meaning on each individual card, there are also patterns based on the colors they display.

Red feathers signify passion. They encourage you to never give up on what you're enthusiastic about, since it keeps you feeling alive and loved on all levels.

Orange feathers signify energy. You should always draw on your power when you are feeling tired and worn out but still want to finish what you've begun. This energy will always be there; you should never take it for granted.

Yellow feathers indicate happiness in your life. They encourage you to expect happiness when you least expect it, as well as to surround yourself with people who make you happy.

Green feathers signify success and health. They indicate that you are one step closer to accomplishing your goals, but must always take care of your health.

Blue feathers indicate boldness. They remind you to never stop doing what you enjoy and to keep going, no matter how many difficulties lie in your way.

Purple feathers signify intuition. They encourage you to trust your gut instincts in all situations and to see and hear the truth beyond what is given and stated to you.

Pink feathers symbolize love. They ask you to recognize that you will always be loved by those you care about and that you should never stop expressing the love you feel.

Brown feathers indicate stability. They urge you to keep your feet on the ground and focus on remaining calm in situations beyond your control.

Gray feathers signify tranquility. They encourage you to seek out tranquility whenever you feel the desire to flee or are on the verge of a breakdown.

White feathers symbolize forgiveness. They encourage you to never retain a grudge that will quickly turn to poison, to forgive but never forget, and to forgive to better yourself and your spirit.

Black feathers are a warning. They also request that you pay great attention to the indications and any clues that things aren't quite right. Don't take any chances and walk away.

Black-and-white feathers signify protection. They remind you that you are constantly being watched over by the Divine and the Cosmos, no matter where you go or what you do.

Spotted feathers reflect a healthy detachment from any material things that are of no value to you. They also symbolize any emotional hurt you need to let go of in order to create space for more extraordinary things to come into your life.

Lined feathers demonstrate that everything is moving in the same direction (whether the lines are vertical or horizontal), and that this is how they should stay to avoid divergence.

If there are multicolored feathers, you can interpret the colors one at a time or pick one that appeals to you. Tones or shades that aren't listed can be interpreted according to your experience of that color. For example, teal may be read as blue or green — the choice is yours.

CARD SPREADS

When the cards are laid out in a spread, they are generally used as a focal point toward a specific topic. Different spreads are available online and in books, or you can create one specific to your needs.

Here are three card spreads that were carefully crafted for this deck. They are offered as a starting point. You can edit the spreads supplied in this guidebook to your taste — for example, you might add, remove, or adjust as many cards as possible. You can also seek alternative spreads you believe are more suitable for your comprehension and reading. As previously mentioned, there are several sources where spreads are available for free.

Single-Card Spread

The single card method is a common way to seek guidance at the beginning of your day. Simply shuffle the cards as you quieten your mind, tuning in to your inner self, and choose one card when your intuition tells you to.

For example, you could ask for a guiding energy for the day, or an indication of what to expect, or what lesson you need to learn today, and so on. You can also use it to get a simple answer to any question.

This method is the most effective way to start learning the cards and how to interpret their meanings, since you will only be analyzing one card.

Past, Present, and Future

This spread is a common way of learning how to combine the meanings of multiple cards into a single, coherent meaning. Quieten your mind and tune in to your inner self as you hold the deck. As you shuffle the cards, contemplate the situation or question you have. When your intuition guides you, choose three cards from anywhere within the deck and lay them out as shown:

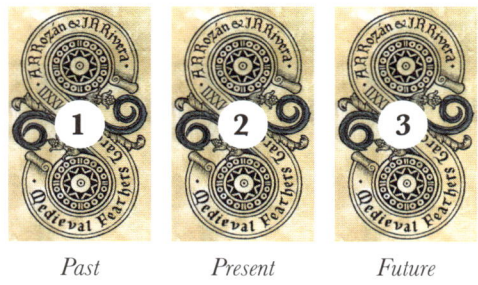

Past   *Present*   *Future*

Card One — *The Distant Past:*
The foundations and past context of the question you ask. Past factors which influence the situation today.

Card Two — *The Present:*
The factors that are entangled with the situation in the present, and influences that could help you choose the direction to take.

Card Three — *The Further Future:*
The possible consequences that may arise from the combination of the past and present.

When you are ready, you can work on the expanded version of this spread below.

The Feather Spread

This simple layout is adapted from a more extensive one developed by the artist, Alejandro R. Rozán. It is an expanded version of the simple Past, Present, and Future spread (above). Looking at the past, the present, and toward the future is an excellent way to understand where you stand in life, which is what this feather-shaped spread will reveal.

Remember that previous energy influences the present, and current energy influences the future. You will have to cope with the power from the future, but there is still time to modify it.

Quieten your mind and tune in to your inner self as you hold the deck. Contemplate the situation or question you have as you shuffle the cards. When your intuition guides you, choose 11 cards from anywhere within the deck and lay them out as shown:

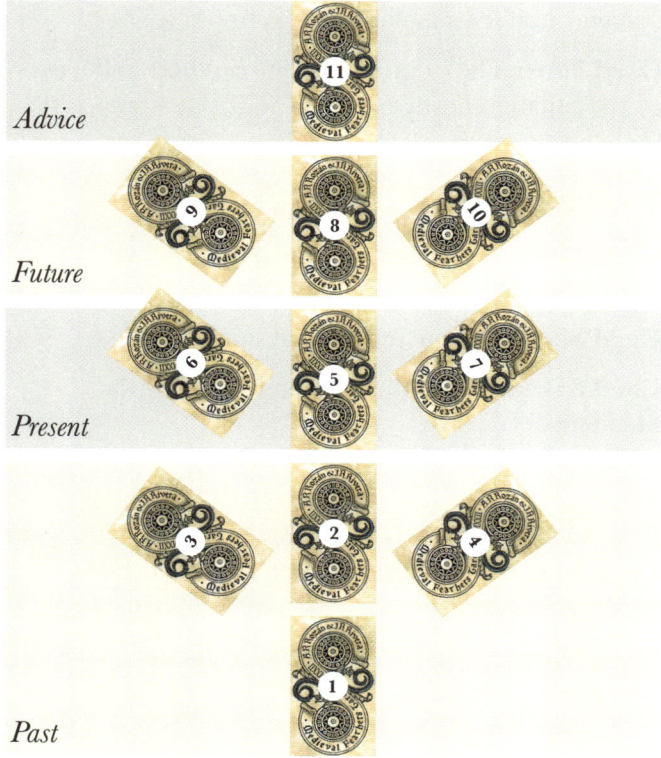

The Past

Card One: The root of the situation

Card Two: An event from the past, which influences the situation

Card Three: The internal/subjective (self) past influences on the situation

Card Four: The external/objective (others) influences on the situation

The Present

Card Five: A description of the present situation as it actually is

Card Six: How you (self) see the situation

Card Seven: How others see and influence the situation

The Future

Card Eight: The likely direction the situation is heading, based on all past and present influences

Card Nine: The possible internal/subjective (self) future influences on the situation

Card Ten: The possible external/objective (others) future influences on the situation

The Advice

Card Eleven: The answer to your question, action, or solution

When you think about it, the medieval imagery and the messages from Heaven provide us with a wealth of knowledge and guidance that we can utilize to improve various aspects of our life. The answers to your questions are within you and are revealed by the cards in this deck. These images, inspired by antique tarot decks once used to pass the time, now reveal glimpses of purpose and fortune.

If you come across a feather on the ground (regardless of its shape or color), pick it up and carry it with you. Give it a particular place in your house, perhaps even set it on an altar you may have and know that the skies have dropped a tiny message for you to decipher and implement in your life.

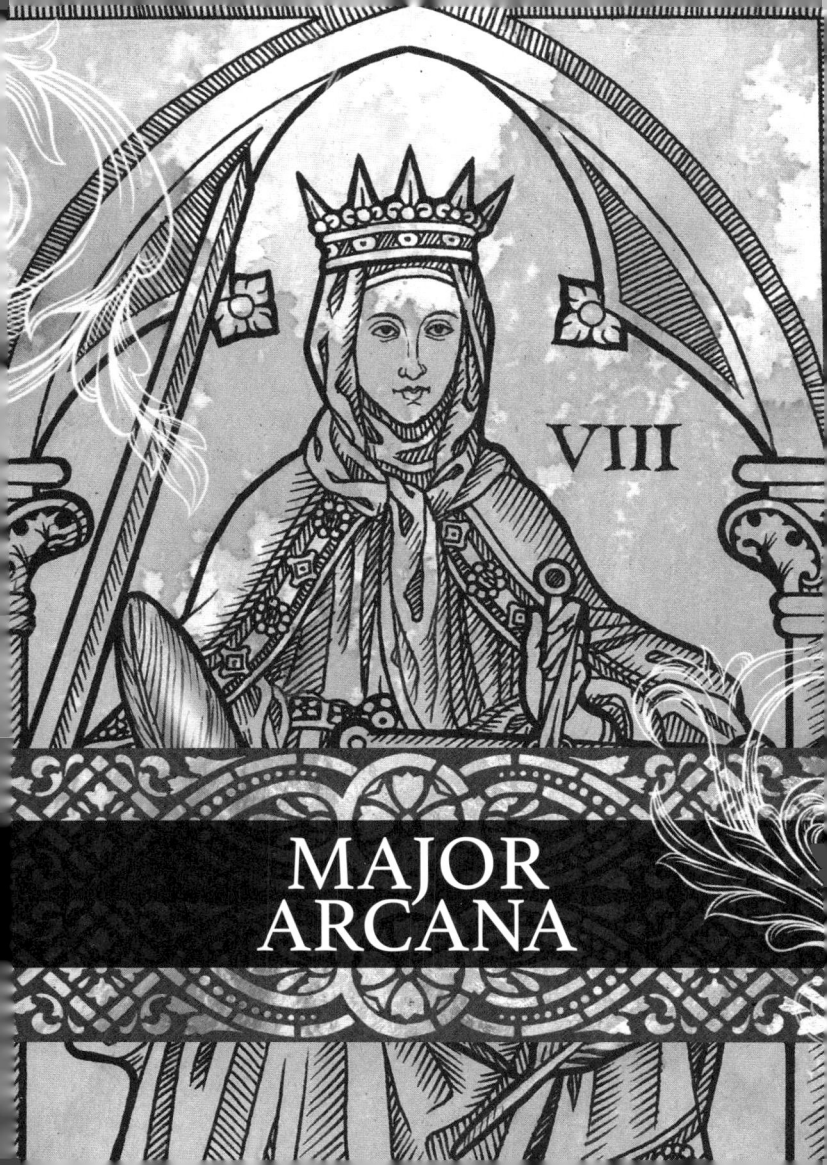

0. LE MAT

0. The Fool

0. THE FOOL - FREEDOM

This poor and inexperienced beginner, expected to amuse people of class and riches, chooses to walk away to maintain his dignity. After his foolishness in front of those who formerly loved his company, no one will ever take him seriously. The parrot's feather tied to the back of his hat is a reminder that he is free to do whatever he wants and go wherever he needs to. His small, faithful companion sees him through the humiliation and attempts to encourage him to run away so he can escape the conditions placed on him to be someone he is not.

Upright Meaning: *Freedom*

Le Mat signifies freedom from everything that pushes you to be someone you are not. It also frees you from making decisions you disagree with. You must remember that you have free will and can do whatever you choose. Therefore, there is no need for you to stay where you are. If you ever doubt the call from within you to move on, don't second-guess it. Let yourself run with the wind and pay close attention to the present moment. Decide what you take into the future and what you will leave behind. Unexpected things will come your way. Receive them without being afraid of what will unfold before you, because there is so much that may benefit you. Life may have set one or more hurdles that hold you back, but the only way to liberate yourself is to conquer them in any manner imaginable.

Reversed Meaning: *Evasive*

You're having trouble committing to a project or a new relationship, and you want to leave it behind so you can run away and do senseless things. It is best for you not to run from it but stay and see how far you can advance. Start to write down ways to approach it, without thinking too hard on it and how much of it you wish to accomplish. By doing so, you will see how the missing pieces will start falling into place.

The Feather

The parrot's feather advises you to abandon old habits and adopt new ones that allow you to explore and discover new things you are curious about.

1. THE MAGICIAN - BEGINNING

I. LE BATELEVR

1. The Magician

He stands behind the wooden table, admiring the stolen tools that rest on it. He tries making sense of them — what exactly can he create out of all those things? Like any ordinary man, he knows he does not possess natural magical abilities. He can't make objects appear and disappear, much less revive a dead creature. He is no ordinary man, however — he is the master of lies, deceit, and manipulation. He can make anyone believe what he pleases. His mischievous monkey rests beneath the table and has been trained to do the same. The feather he holds with his index finger is that of a woodpecker, another creature that makes things disappear for a very long time.

Upright Meaning: *Beginning*

Le Bateleur signifies the time to begin a new craft or project you've imagined. Prepare by gathering the tools you need to create effortlessly and without hassles or hindrances. You may not believe you have the resources, however, look around and see what you already have. Start doing what you need to, without feeling powerless. If you are compelled to share what you're working on—whether under development or completed—please do so. Receiving honest and helpful feedback from others will only lead to the success of your project.

Reversed Meaning: *Conceited*

You are parading around and making a great deal about your work for the sake of attention or fishing for compliments. It's best to keep in mind that there may be flaws in your work and someone else may point them out — this might make you feel incomplete. Be mindful and mind your own business. In turn, this will help you focus on your problems, and how you can save time by resolving them.

The Feather

The woodpecker's feather advises you to look back at any information or details you may have forgotten or overseen. They can be of extraordinary importance to you at this moment.

II. LA PAPESSE

2. The Popess (The High Priestess)

This woman of faith, solid devotion, and profound knowledge sits in her chair, concentrating on interpreting messages from books written by the saints and apostles before her. She is aware of what she knows and understands that everything comes easily for her because of her years of diligent learning. Without hesitation, she writes everything down in her diary with her owl feather's quill, a symbol of great wisdom. She transmits her vast esoteric knowledge onto the pages as she presses the ink on the paper. The contents of her book are secret and not for everybody. Whoever dares to open and read it will not understand it, since it is written in a language she has created. Until someone learns that secret language, all those pieces of information written in her book will not be understood.

Upright Meaning: *Wisdom*

La Papesse indicates the development of your intelligence and intuition. With these higher-order faculties, you don't have to rely on searching for unneeded solutions to grasp perplexing circumstances. Simply sit in silence, concentrate, and think carefully, and let the first impression disclose the truth to better comprehend a situation or see through the deception. When you trust your intuition, you need not second-guess anything. The answers to your questions may take some time to arrive. Remain willing to be patient and embrace the truth, no matter how tough it is.

Reverse Meaning: *Entrench*

You are forced to hide who you are and what you feel and think, because it is demanded of you. This only makes you feel uncomfortable, and you can't find a way to express yourself. Find a hobby, such as writing or painting, which will allow you to express how you feel, and have others read/look at what you've done to get a sense of being heard. This will make you understand how you are able to express yourself, without having to rely on impulses.

The Feather

The owl's feather advises you to never be afraid of what you don't know or understand. When given the opportunity, take the chance to learn new things and discover new avenues. You will find new things you're not familiar with, which can help you in the long run.

III. L'IMPÉRATRICE

3. The Empress

This empress is deemed a mother figure in her empire and sits on her throne between her two servants. Without her orders, her empire cannot establish itself. As she prepares to speak in front of a large audience without her husband's presence, her two humble servants help by holding a large cloth made of silk, reminding her that the empire needs peace and amity. The servant standing in front of her gives her the motivation she needs to keep her mind calm. The servant in front of her shows her an embroidered sheet with a special message she'll address. The servant hiding behind the peacock feather whispers in her ear that the empire is on the verge of falling apart due to misunderstandings and unsolved issues the empire and its people are going through. She will use the advice from her servants to rule her empire and its people with compassion and grace.

Upright Meaning: *Productivity*

L'Impératrice marks the beginning of taking on responsibilities and producing them in the manner that you had envisioned. There is so much to accomplish, but so little time. Now is the time to get started and do as much as possible. As you begin working on any item on your list, you will see how simple it becomes and, consequently, gain new ideas for future tasks. But, of course, take breaks now and again to avoid becoming exhausted.

Reversed Meaning: *Influence*

Be careful when you feel the need—or are influenced—to engage in unethical and risky behaviors that may leave an awkward impression on your peers and friends. Always learn when and how to say, "No," when you feel something is unsafe and against your moral values. In the eyes of others, you may come off as a prude, but you are acting with integrity.

The Feather

The peacock's feather advises you to recognize all the beautiful things which you have accomplished with dignity and grace, and to always do the same.

4. THE EMPEROR - CONTROL

IIII. L'EMPEREVR

4. The Emperor

Sitting on his throne is a man with a strong personality who watches his empire come together. Firmly believing nobody should be alienated, he has established a safe place for everyone to live and co-exist. During his upbringing, he was taught that he is the only person who has control over himself. He will not surrender that power to anyone or anything. Those who dare to attempt to impose any constraint over him will witness his ungodly wrath, which knows no limits. The eagle feather he holds in his hand reminds us that control for the greater good helps to establish structure, and to refrain from becoming possessive.

Upright Meaning: *Control*

L'Empereur knows everything must be completed to avoid setbacks. Whether it is in the workplace or in personal life, ensure nothing is overlooked. Always be confident and strong in what you want to achieve and never allow anyone to get in your way and divert you from

your original objective. Always ensure that you, your
ideas, and everything around you are practical. When
things are steady and regulated, they have a far higher
chance of success than when things are in disarray and
disorder.

Reversed Meaning: *Counsel*

You will have to sort out a dispute or problem that
is bothering you, but you feel you don't have many
options available to you to do so. Never resort to any
actions or words of violence since it will only make
everything much more complicated and cause grave
consequences. If you are ever caught in a situation
like this one, find someone who has dealt with it
before to see what advice they can offer. If you follow
their advice, you will find a solution to most of your
problems, which in turn will give you peace of mind.

The Feather

The eagle's feather advises you to look for answers
to your problems in the places you'd least expect to
find them, and to use them carefully when resolving a
sensitive issue.

V. LE PAPE

5. The Pope (The Hierophant)

This holy man has navigated the world and become cultured in many languages, traditions, and religions. Everything he's learned has had a purpose, and nothing has been in vain. After years of mentoring experience, he knows learning and teaching do not come easy. One has to have discipline and work hard for the results. The cardinal feather he has in his possession signifies he is ready to pass on his vast teachings to the next generation. Everything he knows is ready to be bestowed upon his two disciples who seek his knowledge.

Upright Meaning: *Teachings*

Le Pape signifies it is time to learn something new that has piqued your interest and attention. This is a fresh opportunity to master something new or develop different strategies for ongoing learning. Or, if you find yourself in a challenging scenario, seek the guidance of someone with experience to guide you through it. Be inspired to teach others what you already know. It can be helpful to be a mentor to someone who trusts you so they may learn something new from you, and you can pass on your knowledge and experience as it was passed on to you.

Reversed Meaning: *Expectations*

There are too many rules and regulations you are obligated to follow. Even though it is starting to feel overwhelming, you know you can't just ignore them and do as you please. Instead, find ways to help you adjust to these constraints. Learn what you can gain from following new rules and adjustments, and follow through with them. If you feel nothing important or relevant can be gained from them, it's all right to bend them just a little bit. This will better equip you to deal with constraints.

The Feather

The cardinal's feather advises you to stop following the leader. Instead, be your own leader and follow your dreams and wishes. March to the beat of your own drum.

6. THE LOVERS - ROMANCE

VI. L'AMOVREVX
6. The Lovers

The lovers stand together profoundly in love, fascinated by each other. They wonder who they are now and where their love for one another will take them. Will it be eternal or short lived? They are confused if this is lust or love, but they don't care. The soldier holds a turtledove's feather and gifts it to her. It represents his fascination with her, and she feels the same. The rabbit below their feet represents the purity they embody together. Blindfolded Cupid floats above them, ready to shoot his arrow and seal the deal. Their hearts are racing, prepared to love each other beyond words and unlike they have ever done before.

Upright Meaning: *Romance*

L'Amoureux represents intense feelings of love for someone or something that has captured your heart and made you feel alive. It is a feeling you don't want to end. If you are feeling emotionally and physically alone and require the companionship of another person, search for someone who has chemistry with you, things in common, and allows you to express yourself. When you have a strong desire for someone or something, don't hesitate to take the chance and see where it takes you. If the risk turns out to be favorable, enjoy it while it lasts.

Reversed Meaning: *Inconsistencies*

There are stages in your relationships, whether intimate or familial, where you encounter problems and misunderstandings that seem too difficult to fix, simply because you do not want to deal with whatever is the real problem. The best course of action is to speak about how you feel and what you want to achieve. If you still feel you are getting nowhere, then it's time to end this relationship. Ending it will be painful for you, but it will save you from the struggles that may present themselves in the future. You will also be liberated from dealing with those setbacks.

The Feather

The turtledove's feather advises you to love yourself and remain loyal to yourself and faithful to those in your life. Remember to keep promises you've made to others and yourself, and never give up on the dreams you want to fulfill.

7. THE CHARIOT - SUCCESS

VII. LE CHARIOT

7. The Chariot

This angel of triumph and his two horses of victory have descended from the heavens to attend to all situations with great haste. Seeing how many spend time on senseless activities, he announces that time is running out, and they must do everything to find a way to success. This helps them act, rather than sit, as time goes by. The falcon feather he holds reminds him not to interfere with the choices people make, but he guides them to the appropriate path and guards them. Once he sees that someone is on their way to success, he moves on to the next person who needs his help.

Upright Meaning: *Success*

Le Chariot represents arriving at the achievement you believe was destined for you. Despite the obstacles you had to overcome, nothing stood in your way. Your aspirations have proven legitimate, and you have accomplished all you have ever desired because you felt the determination that drove you over the barriers.

The recognition you want will be yours, since you did everything on your own with little to no assistance — this is something others look up to and seek your guidance on. The next time you find yourself unsure of something good, remember the successful outcome you produced. Keep in mind it won't be your first or last.

Reversed Meaning: *Condescension*

You are starting to show an air of arrogance that is becoming noticed by all those who know you. It is a trait you should keep an eye out for to avoid leaving a wrong impression. When you start to think and feel that you are superior to others, it is one of many signs to look out for. To avoid thinking and feeling like this, it's best to keep your feet on the ground and know all that you have, that you've worked for, can easily be gone. This may sound harsh, but following this will help you evolve as a human being and possibly be a role model for others.

The Feather

The falcon's feather advises you to stay focused on what is important to you and never let anyone drive that attention away from you, no matter what they say or do.

8. JUSTICE - BALANCE

VIII. IVSTICE

8. Justice

This serene yet analytical woman sitting on her throne holds a large, sharp sword in her right hand and a set of scales in her left — necessary tools she needs when deciding on a person's verdict. The sword represents what needs to be severed so peace can be restored, but it can also mean truth, lies, and actions that have grave consequences. The scales signify the ability to find equilibrium in all chaotic situations and where someone's true intentions lie. The crane's feather represents her ability to listen to people speak about their problems and advise what they can do to overcome them.

Upright Meaning: *Balance*

Iustice represents a time when you must find the balance between actions that will lead to the best outcome. How much can you do for yourself? What do you want, and what do you want it for? What do you really want to get out of this? What are the likely consequences? If you ever find yourself in a legal situation, read everything carefully and seek the advice of a professional who can guide and support you through the process. Never let anyone's influence cloud your judgment, and make sure you see a topic or situation for what it is, rather than being affected by other people's viewpoints.

Reversed Meaning: *Liberation*

You may feel as if you are being rather judgmental or biased. See to it that you break away from this and avoid it becoming a habit that you rely on to make rational choices. Accept and tolerate people and things for who and what they are. Understand that everyone and everything has a unique nature. Keep in mind that nothing is ever the same. When you do this, you will feel a sense of freedom from your biases, and your decisions will feel effortless.

The Feather

The crane's feather advises you to do your best by turning any sad moment into a happy one by remembering something valuable, and a lesson that may come from it.

9. THE HERMIT - DETACHMENT

VIIII. L'ERMITE
9. The Hermit

This retired hierophant is undergoing a crisis of faith and is forced to take a breather. He has one important task — to help his troubled soul and restore his confidence. So many before him have tried desperately but failed. Many lost their life doing so, evidenced by his comrade's skull on the floor. Others simply gave up, losing the ability to continue their mission. The eagle owl's feather he holds signifies that his mission will be extended, and he will experience polarizing difficulties such as pain and pleasure, sadness, and happiness. The deer accompanying him reminds him to be aware of his surroundings, since the only aiding tools at his disposal are a lantern and a staff.

Upright Meaning: *Detachment*

Issues have never been resolved because you've pushed them to the back of your awareness, fearing they'll get worse and unmanageable. *L'Ermite* reminds you to seek solutions for these from the only source you can trust — yourself. It is time for you to detach from everything and everyone that consumes your time and attention — they only prevent you from focusing on what is vital and needs attentive consideration. Always remember to be true to your convictions and all you stand for.

Reversed Meaning: *Reclusiveness*

You are spending too much time by yourself to the point where you won't go out or let anybody into your life, causing a great deal of depression you cannot see or manage. Seek like-minded individuals who can help you to acquire the desire to accomplish other things that will give you a sense of purpose. In doing so, you will feel better and a part of the community. Humans are social animals; we require a connection with others to help us feel truly alive.

The Feather

The eagle owl's feather advises you to start tuning in to the mysteries surrounding your everyday life, since those answers can offer some excellent responses that you seek.

10. THE WHEEL OF FORTUNE - CHANGE

X. LA ROVE DE FORTUNE

10. The Wheel of Fortune

The goddess Fortuna has manifested with a mission: to change the force of destiny and luck, and to redeem misfortune and mishaps among those who have lived through much. She is blindfolded, representing her lack of bias when dealing out fortune. As she turns the wheel, it picks up a fast and uncontrollable motion. This will change the fates of those who had nothing and those who had everything. At her indiscriminate whim, the merchant can become king and the king can become a pauper. The robin's feathers illustrate that these men are well aware of her presence and know that things are about to change for them.

Upright Meaning: *Change*

There are numerous changes in circumstances heading your way, and they cannot be tampered with since they are irreversible. That does not mean you cannot adapt and change how you manage change. You need to respond to a new lifestyle, since it's the only way you'll get through difficult times, and this will take time. Every risk, chance, or opportunity you take will not always have a pleasant outcome. If that outcome does not turn out to be what you expected, the best approach is to roll with it.

Reversed Meaning: *Risks*

You are gambling with your health or money and putting yourself—and possibly others—at risk. Be careful when doing this, because it could come with profound, saddening consequences. Be mindful and don't rush into anything you are not experienced with or that feels unsafe; this will help you avoid making any unnecessary mistakes. Protecting yourself and those around you is the best course of action. This, in turn, will help you live a longer and healthier life.

The Feather

The robin's feathers advise you to become more in tune with other people's emotions and feelings, and to understand where they are coming from by trying to relate to them.

11. STRENGTH - POWER

XI. LA FORCE

11. Strength

A youthful woman stands alone inside an empty chamber. Her fears rumble in her stomach and whisper in her ears, attempting to belittle her and leaving her vulnerable. These torments from the past become more powerful, and she cannot stand on her feet. The only pillar in the room provides her with some comfort and support to cling onto. She knows that it can't do much other than sustain her posture. With the cassowary feather, she realizes that eventually she will have to muster the strength to put her mind at ease by facing her fears so that she can stand tall and resilient, just as that pillar does.

Upright Meaning: *Power*

There are tremendous obstacles ahead of you. Now is the moment to gather the courage to fight, for this battle will not be easy. Draw on your inner strength to support you. Using your power rashly can lead to danger or misinterpretation and, on reflection, your intial urges may not feel appropriate. Power is equally about using your strength to act and to refrain from action. When your passion and drive are ready to materialize, bring them out so they can aid you and help you achieve what you need to do in order to make you happy and accomplish whatever you have in mind.

Reversed Meaning: *Uncontrollable*

You are starting to get out of hand, and you're not using your self-control and strength to keep yourself together and composed. This is showing, and once you don't control it, it'll take over and bring you trouble. Think of a difficult moment in your life where you were out of control — what did you do to overcome this tremendous force before it consumed you? Remember the techniques you used, and implement them in what you're facing today. Developing self-control will result in more energy to channel into worthier projects.

The Feather

The cassowary's feather advises that you will have to confront your fears by tackling them head on, with one aim in mind: to liberate yourself from what has been holding you down. Doing this will help you become more resilient, which will help you be more tolerant of things that test your patience.

XII. LE PENDV

12. The Hanged Man

12. THE HANGED MAN - PERCEPTION

This young man has spent his life being conditioned by those who he looked up to and loved dearly. Innocent and naive, he was quick to trust anyone who called him a "friend" and then became easily manipulated. One day, a voice advised him that he could see everything for what it is if he only hung himself upside down from a tree. Believing this divine voice, he dashed to do so. To his surprise, a whirl of revelations displayed like a film before his eyes. Holding the European goldfinch's feather lets him know it's time to see things from another perspective.

Upright Meaning: *Perception*

Le Pendu indicates viewing everything from a different point of view which can only help by seeing the true meaning of things, rather than what you want to see. If you feel what you are dealing with is going nowhere, it's time to understand and accept that something valuable and great will come of it eventually, and in an unexpected way. If you have a habit of seeing what you want to see or if you are influenced by other people's perceptions, then it's time for you to part ways. When you do so, your vision and mind will expand, helping you to see the truth in everything and everyone, which will guide you to resolve difficult issues.

Reversed Meaning: *Ignorance*

You are constantly ignoring your unique qualities and traits. This impacts your life profoundly. You can't be a better person simply because you want to be like those who are admired and loved by society. Don't pretend you're perfect — learn to embrace your imperfections and your whole self by accepting the things you can't change. It's important to live happily. Ignorance of your true nature is why you refuse to accept what is out of your hands. When you understand who you are and behave accordingly, others will begin to treat you the way you've always wished to be treated.

The Feather

The European goldfinch's feather advises you to expand your vision and face the reality you have been avoiding, because it's not going anywhere. This reality will bewitch you until you open your mind and learn to live in it by not being afraid. When you learn to face any realities that seem too harsh for you to bear, you will become more resilient to withstand anything that comes your way.

13. DEATH - ENDINGS

XIII. LA MORT

13. Death

A disgusting skeletal entity travels around Earth with a giant sickle, a tool used to terminate the lives of those whose time is up. He holds a vulture's feather, signifying that death is the only solution to end suffering. This entity is dreaded because there is no escaping it — for those who manage to, he returns eventually to reclaim their soul. Only the worms who feed on his decaying flesh are permitted to touch him. This implies that even after death, something may be left behind after the spirit is gone. When Death appears, people know it is time to say goodbye to everything precious and to learn to let go.

Upright Meaning: *Endings*

You must realize that everything you loved, people you cared about, or things you liked must be let go of. It is time to break away from any old influences that once had a purpose but are now producing overwhelming difficulties that impede your progress and judgment. You must realize that in order to advance and flourish, you must abandon everything you no longer need and replace it with new and exciting things that can benefit you. The best way to let go of something good, like a romance, or something painful, such as heartbreak, is to know that it won't last forever. Everything must end, and the only way to accept this is by slowly transitioning into a state of non-attachment.

Reversed Meaning: *Unforeseen*

An unexpected loss or change has fallen upon you. You're finding it very difficult to move on or even cope with it, which is causing you to remain still and unable to move on and listen to your sadness. Learn to accept your losses and know that it's not the end of the world, although it may feel like it. When you learn to accept what you've lost, then you will be able to move on and start afresh.

The Feather

The vulture's feathers advise you to take insight and learn from past mistakes you have made that have hurt you; this can help you get away from them.

14. TEMPERANCE - RECONCILIATION

XIIII. TEMPÉRANCE

14. Temperance

A beautiful, intelligent chemist has diligently worked on a blended remedy to bring solace to those who are troubled by unbearable hardships of all aspects. The pitcher and liquid represent the source of inspiration she receives from the quail's feather. For so long, she has seen how many people say and do things in the heat of the moment. She would like for people to realize how actions and words can inflict permanent damage when they're not prevented or resolved. This is why she mixes a solution to aid them in resolving their issues, denoting that one must also accept responsibility for the pain they've inflicted on others. The quail's feather symbolizes the need to learn to forgive but never forget, which serves as a lesson.

Upright Meaning: *Reconciliation*

Tempérance represents two things. First, it signifies finding solutions to prevent ruining a connection with someone. It is reconciling with someone that you had a problematic fallout with. Secondly, it illustrates how situations, ambitions, plans, and missions have all taken their toll, leaving you psychologically and physically drained. Now, you must learn to relax and let go of all that energy. If you are under pressure to accomplish a task by a specific date, recognize that you will need patience. Give it time — rushing into it will result in it being undone and incomplete. If in the process you feel like you have neglected yourself, reconcile with yourself by treating yourself to something nice or possibly a vacation. Learn to reconcile and, when you do, you will see how everything will pan out in your favor.

Reversed Meaning: *Equivocate*

You have something significant to finish or accomplish. Yet, you are only going back and forth, without planning how to get anything done or prioritizing what is important for you to do so. This only prolongs the time it could take to complete things. It is time to discipline yourself into finishing what you have started. Learn to balance what you need to do with other outside sources. Try setting some firm boundaries around completing tasks on time. When you stick to these schedules, you will find that you have more energy and, ironically, more time to devote to other pursuits.

The Feather

The quail's feather advises you to stand firm, be self-resilient, and never let anyone or anything push you down, regardless of how much you feel like giving up.

15. THE DEVIL · CONTRADICTIONS

XV. LE DIABLE

15. *The Devil*

This exotic demon is known as the king of lies and deception. He sits on his flames, contemplating and plotting his next plan to cause havoc on innocent lives. The serpent growing out from his body is his muse, giving him ideas on what to do. The bull on his rear spews lies. The hawk on his knee helps him kick away any forces that impose on him. The moth wings denote he is the rightful ruler of hell. So long as he retains the raven's feather and exhales fire, he knows that prayers and magical chants will have no effect on him. On the contrary, this will only make him more robust and powerful.

Upright Meaning: *Contradictions*

This is the perfect time to detach and move on from the trauma, abuse, and pain you have lived with for so long. *Le Diable* is giving you the chance to heal and improve your wellbeing. Express your opinions and how you feel. Never let anyone contradict or feed you misinformation by forcing you to say what they think is convenient to their standards. Don't be tempted to feel as they do. Remember, you have free will to do as you please.

Reversed Meaning: *Realization*

You have been enjoying too much of something that has become a vice, controlling your mental state. Since you are not taking precautions, this is turning into an addiction that will spiral out of control. The best possible way forward is to accept you have a problem and stop living in denial. It's time to seek the support you need from someone capable of helping you through the process. This is not a sign of weakness, but a show of strength, humility, and vulnerability. When you realize that you need outside help, the help will come. You will soon discover that there is so much more you are capable of.

The Feather

The raven's feather advises that you will go through some unfamiliar and unexpected changes that seem frightening but will be a good cause in your life. The best source of preparation for what's to come is to not dwell on it but embrace it when it manifests.

16. LIGHTNING · FORTUITY

XVI. LA FOUDRE

16. Lightning

La Foudre—lightning—is precisely what this man has seen and was lucky enough not to get struck by. He sits under the tree, which represents growth and is an omen of opposing sides. The lightning served a purpose — it caused his lambs to gather into one place, safe from the threat of predators. This signifies gentleness in times of desperation. The mighty phoenix's feather lets him know the lightning was a message from God — be prepared to detach from all things that hold purpose for him, as there will be other things to come.

Upright Meaning: *Fortuity*

It is time for you to break free from any constraints—physical or mental—that are limiting you from doing what you want and discovering new things to appreciate. You're on your way to achieving a breakthrough in what you've spent time learning and working on. Once you break through, you'll feel committed to your tasks and goals. If you ever desire to return to the way you used to enjoy things and what made you feel at ease, know that it is never too late to return and remain there, no matter what.

Reversed Meaning: *Stagnation*

You have not been careful with your projects and personal problems. Because of this, everything you have tried to achieve will remain idle, unable to progress. You will have to leave things as they are and come back to them at another time to proceed. Gathering advice from others to help you continue from where you stopped, and possibly rebuilding everything from nothing, may just prove useful.

The Feather

The phoenix's feather advises that everything motionless will soon animate itself and come to life, showing you that anything is possible if you only believe.

XVI. LA MAISON DIEV

16. The House of God (The Tower)

16. THE HOUSE OF GOD - EMANCIPATION

An angry god has struck the roof of a tower, freeing his disciple who has been held hostage by heretics because of his pure heart and his inability to refuse humanitarian services to anyone. The disciple knew the time was near. Seeing the phoenix feather emerge out of the flames, he is at peace with the destruction, knowing there is a sacred reason for his god's anger. As he plummets to the ground, he does not know what his fate will be after his descent — will he find eternal rest up in the heavens or live to tell his ordeal? For now, he is glad to have avoided an unjust punishment. He knows deep in his heart that he will survive this fall and use his experience to free others from similar situations.

Upright Meaning: *Emancipation*

You have been bound to someone or something and now have the opportunity to break free, without looking back. Too many trials and difficulties have taken their toll on you, but all of that is now behind you. Now, you may find solace and serenity. If you've been urgently attempting to break into something new—a profession or pastime—anticipate that it will go as planned, and you will find your way into it. You've earned it. Breaking away may seem awkward initially, but once you take control of your life, it will become much more manageable.

Reversed Meaning: *Precaution*

Be cautious of how you do things; everything you have worked so tirelessly for will soon be crumbling at your feet, and there is no way to rebuild it. A position you hold may be taken from you if you cannot conduct yourself properly and professionally. Pick up good examples from people who are well-behaved and professional. Seek their advice when you are confused about certain things. You will start to see how everything plays out for you in the end.

The Feather

The phoenix's feather advises you that everything which was once motionless will soon animate itself and come to life and show you that anything is possible if you only believe.

17. THE STAR - VISIBILITY

XVII. L'ESTOILLE

17. The Star

A gleaming star in the night sky has entrusted a knowledgeable astronomer with the capacity to assist others in discovering their true intentions and potential for more tremendous success. At times, it was difficult for him to convey who he was without being condemned and dubbed cruel names, especially as an old man who sat peering into space with his telescope. The lovely swan's feather helps him identify those who suffer the most and the remedies they need to live happily with who they are. He works with them to discover the bravery they require. Once his task is over, he will assign a star to that individual as a continual reminder to never be influenced by the opinions and ideas of others.

Upright Meaning: *Visibility*

You feel upset or as if nobody is there to listen to you during difficult times. Start being yourself and stop hiding from the world for the sake of being on good terms with those who can't accept you. Accept that your true self has value and a lot to offer others.

Be true to yourself and understand what you need and how you can receive it. When a situation seems too good to be true, keep your feet on the ground and never let it get to your head. You will need a clear mind to think of what to do when it is all over. Your true self has much more value and much to offer others.

Reversed Meaning: *Perilous*

You are engaging with strangers displaying risky behaviors and attitudes, and thus you are failing to set strict and safe boundaries for yourself. It would be best if you started with sensing any potential danger. By doing this, you may find yourself not needing to deal with other people's faults and problems.

The Feather

The swan's feather advises you to look for all the things you thought were unattractive and useless, and to see their true beauty and value. This will be one of many ways you will learn to appreciate the smaller but simplest things in life.

18. THE MOON - EMOTIONS

XVIII. LA LUNE

18. The Moon

The luminescent moon brightens the dark lonely night and surrounds a young peasant woman weaving hay. She is doing her best to get in touch with her emotions. For so long, she has been oppressed by the men in her life and forced to keep her feelings to herself, since they were not considered to be of any importance nor serve a useful purpose. Unable to bottle in her feelings any longer, she has asked the moon to help her release them so she can understand their meaning. As she weaves away, and with the magpie's feather present, her consciousness drifts to another plane, and she taps into her unconscious to reflect on the issues troubling her.

Upright Meaning: *Emotions*

La Lune signifies your capacity to delve deeper into emotions you haven't acknowledged, which have so many unique and essential things to tell you. You have recently been dreaming of gaining what you've been told is unattainable, but you know one day you will be able to obtain it. The solutions to the problems you've been looking for are within you, but you haven't taken the effort or commitment to go and get them because you expect them to come to you. Sit, be silent, and close your eyes; concentrate on the first feeling you feel. When you are able to tap into your emotions, the solution to your problems rests in your hands.

Reversed Meaning: *Escape*

You are picking up on a lot of negativity coming from people around you, and it's starting to affect your state of mind. You are starting to feel and think in ways you are not used to. Do not let these feelings and thoughts get the best of you. Go out and enjoy doing what you like the most. Remember, you can't control how others think or feel — only how you do. Tune out the opinions of others and instead focus on the encouraging thoughts and feelings within your being.

The Feather

The magpie's feather advises you to not take any arguments or disagreements to heart and learn to solve them with integrity and tranquility, without becoming too aggravated. This, in turn, will help you understand that life isn't as difficult as you thought it would be.

19. THE SUN - BLESSINGS

XVIIII. LE SOLEIL

19. The Sun

This radiant sun shining with all its glory and granting unlimited amounts of blessings has bestowed a mission on an honest woman to be the one to deliver its benefits. She knows what it is like to work hard and not be acknowledged for it, and the heartbreak, frustration, and sadness it brings. Before blessings can be delivered, and with the rooster's feather, she has to ensure that the person asking for them is worthy and that their heart is pure, and intentions are clear. Once the person earns their blessings, they will have to return the favor to someone who requires help, so it too can multiply.

Upright Meaning: *Blessings*

Le Soleil represents everything you like doing. Everything which surrounds you brings nothing but warmth, light, and happiness, even when you feel lost and alone. This is the time to be joyful and appreciative for all you've gained through hard work and dedication. Keep the people you love close because they're the reason this happiness surrounds you. The sense of being delighted with your mental and physical wellbeing will continue for a long time, and you can share your shining positivity with others less fortunate. When you share these traits, you are opening your doors to receiving help when you are feeling lost and alone, and your own blessings will be your antidote.

Reversed Meaning: *Resolution*

You are having a rather difficult time facing the reality of worsening situations that are causing a disturbance in your life and peace. You must realize that they will not go away on their own, and you will have to deal with them accordingly. Until you are able to fix this, you will be dealing with a lack of enthusiasm and unrealistic expectations. Once these problems have the light of reality shone on them, you will find it easier to think clearly and rationally about how to resolve these issues.

The Feather

The rooster's feather advises you to wake up and realize that there is much more to do and take advantage of to improve your life. This, in turn, will help you become independent and self-sufficient.

20. JUDGMENT - REVELATION

XX. LE IUGEMENT

20. *Judgment*

A celestial entity has descended to revive those who met their quick demise without being able to fulfill their goals. The golden trumpet produces beautiful notes that serenade the corpses and inject new life into their empty bodies. Holding a pelican's feather, the angel reveals that they will no longer be the same people they used to be. They will be starting their new lives afresh, and they will have to acquire new memories and make new lives for themselves. They agree to whatever conditions are given, as long as they can be alive and thrive as they intended before life was taken away.

Upright Meaning: *Revelation*

Le Iugement represents something you have been seeking for a long time — only you know what it is. It will eventually appear, and you will have to grasp it before it disappears. Any physical or mental pain you have undergone, whether caused by someone else or yourself, will be relieved fast. The healing process will be short and will not leave you feeling immobilized. Whatever it was that didn't make sense to you, whether it was someone else's secrets or your own issues, new and profound knowledge will make itself visible in your mind and you will be able to recognize its truth.

Reversed Meaning: *Persistence*

When the answers you are looking for are not at your disposal, your best bet is to remain motivated and hopeful. Keep pushing through until you are able to see what you need, not what you want. Should it not manifest, step away and let it come to you. By letting go of your attachment to the answers you seek, you create the space to allow them to arrive naturally and unforced. Keep your mind open to the infinite possibilities.

The Feather

The pelican's feather advises you to stop putting other people's needs before your own, see what you need to do appropriately, and continue to be happy. When you put your needs first, this will teach you to value yourself and ensure you are content.

21. THE WORLD - COMPLETION

XXI. LE MONDE

21. The World

This woman is known to bring success and prosperity to everyone who works so hard and tirelessly. Within her emerges the next generation, whom she will nurture and educate to bring healing and good fortune to the world. She knows this young child has much potential to do great things, which is why she will invest in her. Two divine angels blow a breath of fresh air at her so there can be divine intervention should any troubles arise when initiating this task, since this is very delicate and should not fail. The pheasant's feather will be the source of inspiration to help the child complete its mission.

Upright Meaning: *Completion*

Le Monde signifies how much time and effort you have invested on a project that has finally come to completion. Now, you can finally step back and admire everything you have done, without doubting whether you did it correctly. By doing this, you will realize that anything you want to do and finish in life may not be easy, but, most importantly, will be possible. There will be no doubt in your mind that you are capable of doing so much more. Remember that this may seem like a final completion, but there is much more to come, and you have to be ready to set out and do it.

Reversed Meaning: *Disconnect*

You tend to make it a habit to live in the world disconnected from everyone and everything. At times, you refuse to acknowledge what others have to say, which could actually be beneficial to you. It is time for you to open up to the different things that are out there in the world. This, in turn, will help you to understand that there is so much more to life than living in your own bubble. Just because you feel the world is a scary place, it doesn't mean there isn't something valuable in it for you — you just need to find it within yourself to go out there and seek it.

The Feather

The pheasant's feather advises you to stop ignoring your physical and emotional needs and start giving yourself what you need to replenish yourself and your wellbeing. By taking care of yourself, you are giving yourself the chance to be healthy, to grow, and understand that you matter.

XXII. LE CONSULTANT

22. The Querent

The dragon gnawing at its tail represents the never-ending cycles spirits must go through. Encircled by it is an androgynous human representing all genders. The zodiac signs are depicted vertically along their body. This person is floating in the sky, maybe even in space. The hummingbird's feather represents their ability to set their feet firmly on the ground and flourish once they have found answers to their problems. This card can represent the querent: the subject of the tarot reading. *Le Consultant* will remain in this position until they have found the answer to their question. It can also be included in the deck and used for divinatory purposes.

22. THE QUERENT - SELF-EMBODIMENT

Upright Meaning: *Self-embodiment*

Le Consultant highlights the importance of appreciating and integrating every part of your being that contributes to who you are — both inner and outer. You are fully aware of your flaws and weaknesses, but this has nothing to do with what you can achieve with your enormous potential. While you believe there is far too much to fix within yourself, you should focus on learning to love who you are, regardless of what others think. When you do this, you will notice that everyone else also sees it, and you may even begin to encourage others to follow in your footsteps.

Reversed Meaning: *Neglect*

Problems have pushed you to the point where you are neglecting yourself, tarnishing your image and your health, which is very unlike you. Pressure from the outside and other people's negative influences are hindering what you can do for yourself. If you find yourself in this type of situation, come up with a plan where you can separate from it. Look for help and advice from people who have been through similar experiences. When you are able to collect useful and helpful information, apply it to yourself and you will see that this hold will no longer consume you.

The Feather

The hummingbird's feather advises you to keep a close eye on your surroundings and people in your circle, since they require a friend who can hear them out.

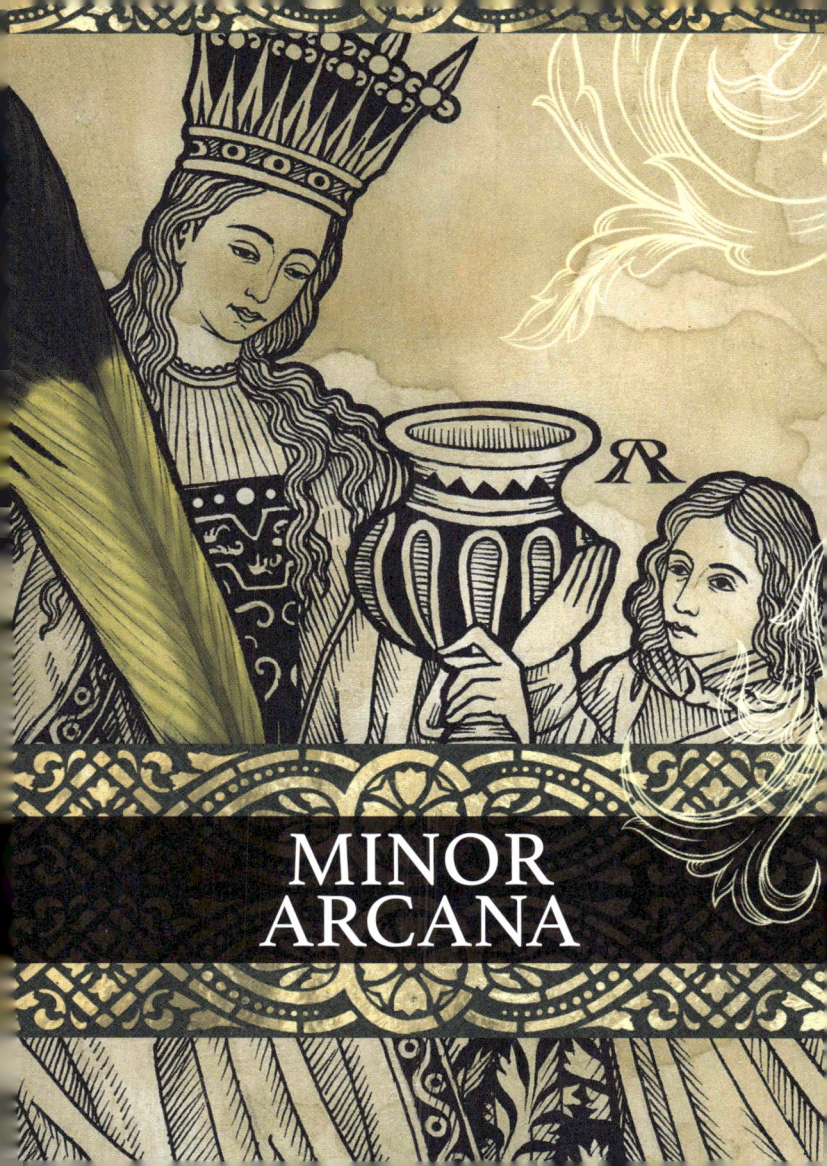

MINOR ARCANA

LES DENIERS

The suit of *Deniers* represents the material and physical aspects of life, such as the physical body, material wealth, and all that is practical and conservative. In conventional tarot, this is the suit of Coins, Pentacles, or Disks.

Take a coin from your purse and invest it in your mind. It will come pouring out of your mind and overflow your purse.

—Benjamin Franklin

ACE OF COINS - MATERIAL

AS DE DENIER

Ace of Coins

This beautiful and gentle unicorn is responsible for granting hard workers material wealth, on the condition that she's taken care of. She does not give rewards in vain, and those who seek material gain for hidden agendas are in for a rude awakening. Aside from material things, she bestows excellent fortune to those in dire need, since she knows it will be spent for good use. The blue tit's feather reminds the unicorn that those who are pure of soul will have the providence to see her manifest in a person, which is a sign that they are to expect beautiful things soon.

Upright Meaning: *Material*

As de Denier indicates a critical moment of responsibility for your financial and physical wellbeing. For a long time, you have been learning to become physically and financially secure, and it supports you in taking care of yourself by avoiding any unpleasant setbacks. You will be comfortable and safe for a very long time if you concentrate on your wellbeing without worrying about irrelevant issues. This is a turning point in your life — don't allow anything to derail or sabotage it. You are far too important and must learn to be happy.

Reversed Meaning: *Avarice*

Due to your experiences of being taken advantage of, you have closed yourself from sharing what you have with others. Although others may call you stingy and selfish, you only do this to be able to preserve what little you have left. In other people's eyes, this may be an act which is frowned upon. But for you, this is survival. Don't let this take a hold of you, since sharing what you have may benefit others and possibly the favor will be returned to you. Learn to share in moderation, and if someone demands too much, refrain from doing so.

The Feather

The blue tit's feather advises you to find all the means possible to reach your goals, even when you have to make sacrifices to get to where you want to be. Though it may seem difficult at first, keep in mind that you are only making room to manifest the things you're anticipating.

DEUX DE DENIER

Two of Coins

TWO OF COINS - CHOICE

Two coins rest on top of one another for support. They show each other that they are there for one another. The band that holds them together comes close to forming the infinity sign, meaning the bond will be unbreakable. The flowers grow out of the two coins to give them what they need to keep spinning and to keep their value intact. The Wilson's bird-of-paradise feather helps the two coins to take charge.

Upright Meaning: *Choice*

Deux de Denier signifies that you are given two distinct alternatives to pick from that will help you with whatever is bothering you. With this, you may apply it where it is most required and utilize it to your advantage to complete any unfinished tasks. In certain circumstances, one choice will overwhelm the other, forcing you to choose the one that benefits you. However, you may save the second one for when it is needed. Remember that you will only have two, so invest carefully.

Reversed Meaning: *Mediation*

A decision needs to be made, and you are taking a long time to come to one, which will only hinder any plans you have set out for yourself. Once these options disappear, there is no other way to retrieve them. Avoid thinking too deeply on the matter at hand and set your intention to find a way to resolve the conflicting choices. The upside is that by discovering this technique of mediating between your indecision, you will be able to apply it to future problems.

The Feather

Wilson's bird-of-paradise drops its feather to advise you to let loose and not be so uptight. Avoid taking things too seriously — life is meant to be enjoyable. Learn to relax and have some fun if and when the time calls for it. When you learn to relax, you're giving your mind a break from the harshness it has been put through.

THREE OF COINS · ASSOCIATION

TROIS DE DENIER

Three of Coins

The three coins are responsible for producing what is needed for all things to have value. The coin on top of the other two oversees that everything is being done correctly and accordingly so there will be no setbacks and things won't lose their value. The other two coins at the bottom will support the one at the top, so everything turns out fine. These coins receive support from the canary's feather.

Upright Meaning: *Association*

Trois de Denier allows collaboration with someone experienced and trustworthy on a project or anything else. To see positive outcomes, the alliance you formed with that individual must be honest, open, and good-natured. There must be no hidden agendas between you and anyone else. If you both realize the unlimited possibilities, working together will be less challenging and more fun and fruitful. This will allow you to form a more powerful, unbreakable bond and trust that cannot be severed.

Reversed Meaning: *Redemption*

Now is when you'll have to make things right and fix plans which you left unattended in order to avoid disappointment with the results. But you may also be the one who, with your lack of tactics, will leave others disappointed. First and foremost, own up to your mistakes and admit you did wrong. Try your best to undo what you've done but make it heartfelt. This, in turn, will show others your sincerity, and trust will be restored.

The Feather

The canary's feather advises you to be competent in everything you do and not let others dismay you otherwise. Always remember not to be your own harsh critic but to accept and embrace when you need help learning something new.

QUATRE DE DENIER

Four of Coins

FOUR OF COINS - STABILITY

These four coins are placed neatly on each corner and represent the notion of being stable. They have everything running smoothly, without worrying about anything interfering. In their placement, they resemble the four cardinal elements: earth, fire, air, and water. The goose's feather helps the four coins to remain firm and stable.

Upright Meaning: *Stability*

Quatre de Denier signifies that you've been able to stabilize your plans, and others will acknowledge and praise your hard work because of your devotion and sacrifices. They will honor you for your dedication and high ethics, which you have demonstrated to everyone around you through being grounded and firm. Stability allows you opportunities and resources to achieve more extraordinary things. Still, you must know when and how to use these, since they may only come to you once. As a result, you will never underestimate your potential or what you are capable of.

Reversed Meaning: *Attention*

Your attention is not being placed where it needs to be, nor is it taking notice of all the things that are falling apart in your life. This is the time to push everything that's irrelevant aside and focus on what's important. Doing this will help you prevent more things from piling up, and you will slowly see how this will be beneficial for you.

The Feather

The goose's feather advises you to hold on tightly to all that you have worked very hard for, because you may be on the verge of losing it all at the hands of a person with ill intentions. Once it is lost, it will be complicated to regain it. Holding on to your achievements will serve as a reminder that you can do anything you set your mind to.

FIVE OF COINS - INTERFERENCE

CINQ DE DENIER

Five of Coins

As with the previous image, the four coins were perfectly placed at the corners of the card. Here, another coin is added which disrupts the perfect pattern made from the four coins. The fifth coin now stands alone in the center of the card, ruining the stability of the four coins. The stellar jay's feather helps to manage the disruption of peace.

Upright Meaning: *Interference*

Cinq de Denier signifies any new energy or circumstance that is too powerful to manage and appears to be getting out of hand. Now is the moment to figure out how you will handle it, since it can upset your stability and wreak havoc. You'll have to pay close attention, because it's utterly unknown to you and will force you out of your comfort zone. However, this will help you become much more aware of new developments.

Reversed Meaning: *Lessons*

You lack the courage to face any interference that has made its way into your personal space. This only serves to delay your plans, which you have tried hard to bring together. To find the courage you need, learn from someone you admire, be they in your life or from history. Study how they came to be brave, and apply their lessons in your life. Use their example as a model of how to deal with unexpected difficulties. When you do so, you will find it easier to face disruptions in your life and you will learn valuable lessons from them.

The Feather

The stellar jay's feather advises that if you are ill, you must find a way to care for yourself, even if it means giving up important things such as a job or a relationship. Your wellbeing comes first. Once you are in better health, you may set out and resume the relationship that was placed on pause and maybe you'll find a better job. Trust that this is not the end; it is just the beginning.

SIX OF COINS - EXPANSION

SIX DE DENIER

Six of Coins

Six coins have gathered around in aligned locations without seeming weird or out of place. They have multiplied and are now grouped in threes, visible to all. They are soothing on the eyes, but not bombarding nor boring to look at. The hornbill's feather helps them to expand.

Upright Meaning: *Expansion*

Everything you set your mind to may become even more incredible than you expected, and you've arrived at the moment you've been waiting for. This is the ideal time to get started on what you desire, and watch it grow before your eyes. Despite what you may be going through, there is always room for you to put effort into this endeavor, so don't be scared to go out into the world. Once it is under development, you will be inspired to begin working on new and intriguing projects that you will like. This, in turn, will help you expand your horizons to new and exciting things.

Reversed Meaning: *Tentative*

You lack a positive outlook on the success you have worked for, and you feel you need more. Now, you are becoming eager to acquire more than you can obtain and handle. This leaves you restless, and it means nothing around you feels complete. The best advice is to take things slowly, one step at a time. Expansion is slower, but at least it will happen surely and slowly over time. This will leave room for you to undertake other tasks you're anticipating.

The Feather

The hornbill's feather advises you to give something to someone you know is struggling through hardship. This can be as simple as a piece of clothing or a small amount of money. Make it heartfelt, and do it because you feel it within you. Not only will the person feel good about it, but so will you. It will leave a long-lasting impression.

SEVEN OF COINS · ACCEPTANCE

SEPT DE DENIER

Seven of Coins

Within this image there are seven coins. Even though seven is an odd number, the coins are grouped in two different arrays. One is an odd number consisting of three coins, while the other is an even number of four. Although they don't match, they learn to adapt with the help of the colorful lark's feather in between them all.

Upright Meaning: *Acceptance*

What others offer you—regardless of its worth or nature—must be embraced as a gesture of appreciation. This may help you pay off any debts you have. Accept and acknowledge when you are suffering, and take any aid offered to you. What is being offered to you may also be helpful for others who may be struggling. The good news is that you are not required to repay it — it is yours to keep. What you will learn and teach others from this is to accept when help is needed without feeling ashamed. There is a reciprocity here that benefits everyone.

Reversed Meaning: *Dependence*

Lately, you have felt like you are struggling with all you need to achieve, and this has lowered your self-esteem. You've begun to feel helpless and useless to yourself and others. But it isn't because you are useless, but because you depend on the acknowledgment of those around you — which you realize you haven't been receiving. Stop depending on others and learn ways to help yourself. This will train you to become self-reliant whenever you face similar or different obstacles.

The Feather

The lark's feather advises you to start thinking about the changes you need to make in your life. Imagine how you will get used to them and how they can benefit all areas of your life in the long run. There is no room for worrying, just enough time to get prepared for what's in store for you in the future.

EIGHT OF COINS - GROUNDING

HUIT DE DENIER

Eight of Coins

There are eight coins — four on each side that are perfectly aligned with each other. This is the beginning of a solid, sturdy, unbreakable structure that is starting to form. The Eurasian tree sparrow's feather in the middle makes the third column to even out everything, so they remain untouched.

Upright Meaning: *Grounding*

Huit de Denier shows your capacity to approach issues that demand your attention. You can carefully complete tasks at a reasonable pace, without overworking yourself. Never rush into anything without fully understanding what needs to be done and how to execute it — doing so will only set you up for failure. This will help you develop strategies that will enable you to get out of tight circumstances when you don't have a way out, and that will be useful the next time you work on something similar. Anything you do must have a human touch and be grounded in reality rather than fantasy.

Reversed Meaning: *Hastiness*

You are rushing into things without thinking about them first. This lack of good judgment leads to consequences that are less than favorable — at worst, they can be disastrous. There is no way to go back and fix the mistakes, you can only mitigate the effects of your actions. Make the effort to learn from all of this and prepare yourself to avoid repeating the same mistakes again. Wisdom comes from applying the knowledge you've learned to everyday situations.

The Feather

The Eurasian tree sparrow's feather advises you to increase your knowledge, whether in what you already know or new endeavors. What you will understand in the future will serve as a valuable asset anywhere you go and to those you encounter.

NINE OF COINS - MOTIVATION

NEUF DE DENIER

Nine of Coins

These nine coins work independently without having to rely on each other. The only common factor they share is the motivation they provide each other to get through difficult situations. With this, they are able to do so much more than they imagined. The guinea fowl's feather, which stands in between, pushes all the coins to unite and cheer up each other so they can understand their worth.

Upright Meaning: *Motivation*

When you are fatigued and want to give up, seek out those who can bring motivation into your life. Needing to perform several tasks at once without any energy will be near impossible and will drain you even more. The quality of your work will also suffer. Having someone who can help and motivate you leads to better outcomes for each task and your ability to sustain yourself over time. You can still be ambitious, as long as you're doing it with good intentions and some friendly backup because this will benefit you in the long run. Remember that putting as much effort as you can into anything will have a longer-lasting effect.

Reversed Meaning: *Drive*

You are not tapping into your drive, which can take you places and help you do so many things that you've always wanted to. This is turning into a pattern you refuse to acknowledge. Thus, you can't do what you need to succeed. It's time to switch gears. Reflect on when you had the energy and motivation to get things done. What did it feel like in your body? Bring back this feeling now, and summon the courage to get out there and do your best.

The Feather

The guinea fowl's feather advises you to seek ways to feel better about yourself and all that you have achieved, without having to rely on what others say. Giving in to people's unwanted feedback will take away from enjoying the small things in your life.

TEN OF COINS · ABUNDANCE

DIX DE DENIER

Ten of Coins

Fortunate are those who have ten powerful coins — they have the power to multiply one's abundance. Two groups of five coins are arranged from top to bottom that will unite and grant a handsome amount of wealth. The black-headed gull's feather, rich in color, denotes all the wonderful things that can be granted to those who bestow it.

Upright Meaning: *Abundance*

Dix de Denier signifies the tremendous quantity of abundant resources available to you to help improve your finances and everything else you value. Be careful how and where you spend it. This abundance is available to you—tangible and not—to share with those in need of some good in their life. You'll see how good that will make you feel. If you wisely invest, you can be confident that you will be safe in all aspects of your life, and nothing can take that away from you. Then you won't have to worry about not having enough of anything.

Reversed Meaning: *Investment*

Everything that you have worked for and everything you've received is being wasted on careless choices and impulses. You've been investing your time, energy, and money on useless things that serve no purpose, as opposed to taking care of them. You need to be aware of where you spend your hard-earned money. Be sure to save some for a rainy day. You may find you are pleasantly surprised at how much you can accumulate.

The Feather

The black-headed gull's feather advises you to seek ways to make something you've been working on sustainable over a long time. To see lasting results in your endeavors should be at the forefront of your mind. This will, in turn, outline what is important to you, and by attending to it, it will give you a sense of completion. This will help you avoid resorting to what does not provide for you.

PAGE OF COINS - POTENTIAL.

VALET DE DENIER

Page of Coins

This young and bubbly woman was deemed someone who would never have a breakthrough in what she aspired to. Everyone thought she would conform to how society views young women — find a husband, bear children, and be a homemaker. Deep down inside, she knows there is far more than that and understands there's a way to prove it to herself. The gold coin she holds in her hand helps her to value her worth. Although the road may prove difficult initially, she will eventually reach her full potential. The great bittern's feather reminds her there will be no turning back since she has a long way to go.

Upright Meaning: *Potential*

When *Valet de Denier* appears in a situation, it provides an opportunity to strike out and seek chances that will help you grow as an individual to help you stand out from the rest of the crowd. What you find can also help you make all of your dreams a reality without having to rely on others.

As an archetype, the valet signifies someone who looks for the perfect time to seize opportunities, without settling for anything less. The person she represents seeks to learn everything they can about business and finance to become an ideal ally.

Reversed Meaning: *Unmotivated*

This is a situation where you feel you need more confidence. This attitude is holding you back — you are slowly becoming uptight, moody, and unable to do anything for yourself.

Reversed, *Valet de Denier* represents an archetype who lacks clear motives and purposes. When trying to help someone out, they cause setbacks to everyone around them and ruin anything they get involved in.

The Feather

The great bittern's feather tells you to be as practical as possible. This begins with suitable methods in everything you do and wherever you go, since putting both feet on the ground will motivate you to achieve much more than you thought.

KNIGHT OF COINS - DIRECTION

CAVALIER DE DENIER

Knight of Coins

This lovely and gallant young man stands firm with his paws on the ground. There, he feels the energy of everyone living and deceased and starts communicating with those who have passed away. He holds a gold coin in his hand, made through the elements gathered from the earth's minerals. Being grounded, he plants roots to help those who are lost, providing them with the direction they need to find what they seek. With the American bald eagle's feather, he has the foresight and wisdom to know what to do and where to go.

Upright Meaning: *Direction*

Cavalier de Denier points you in a one-way direction that will help maintain order in your life. When you pursue this path to the very end, you will discover the tools you need to continue to progress, and there will be no turning back.

As an archetype, *Cavalier de Denier* signifies someone always willing to give help and guidance. When they see someone struggling, they make it their goal to help them get through it.

Reverse Meaning: *Derailing*

Cavalier de Denier reversed suggests you are losing your way. Getting back on track will be complicated if you don't act fast and set your priorities straight. Take a moment to reflect on where you are and where you are heading and discover what you may need to help you back on your journey. This archetype represents someone who takes things and people for granted and meddles in personal affairs to set up someone for failure.

The Feather

The American bald eagle's feather advises you to stay realistic in what you do and think. Avoid daydreaming, since you need both your feet planted on the earth in order to be in touch with reality. On a difficult day, it's okay to wander off, so long as you bring yourself back to reality and get on with things.

REYNE DE DENIER

Queen of Coins

The rightful ruler knows precisely where she stands, and never deviates from her role. The golden coin she holds lets everyone know she has a keen eye for knowing who is practical and who is apathetic. Holding the great egret's feather reminds her to play her role as a benevolent and prudent ruler. The young woman who stands by her side is her personal and loyal servant. To gain her position, she had to prove herself worthy, and it took a long time to acquire. As the queen, her superiors harshly trained her to bring tact and fairness to all who surrounded her.

Upright Meaning: *Practicality*

Drawing this card signifies one needs to be grounded when doing activities that must be handled seriously. Fooling around will only lead to stagnation. Finding a means to work effectively might give you a sense of calm and happiness in your job.

As an archetype, it represents someone who is rooted on all levels, appreciates offering excellent counsel, and looks after others. This is someone everybody may rely on, without feeling embarrassed or humiliated any time they need assistance or direction.

Reversed Meaning: *Materialism*

Reyne de Denier reversed tells you that you are only looking at material things because of their monetary value and how much you could earn from them. She wants you to truly cherish what you value.

As an archetype, it denotes a person who is selfish, self-centered, and possessive. They enjoy manipulating others to their amusement. Only what is important to them matters.

The Feather

The great egret's feather advises you to nurture everything, including yourself, by not neglecting your needs as well as the needs of others. There will come a place and time when you won't be able to do it all, and there is nothing wrong with that. This is a sign to stop what you're doing and take needed rest so you can come back to it refreshed.

KING OF COINS - PRINCIPLES

ROY DE DENIER

King of Coins

The king is incredibly wealthy and opulent, and he realizes it took a long time to get what he has. He doesn't waste any time, as depicted by the coin in his grasp. He puts off traveling and spending lavishly because he understands there is a far more critical situation that needs immediate attention, and only he can resolve it. When something or someone is a priority, he knows very well who to lean on, trusting them to aid him. But when someone is judged untrustworthy, all he needs to do is remove them from his court to prevent any misinterpretation. He carries the belted kingfisher's feather, which advises him to recognize pressing problems are more pressing.

Upright Meaning: *Principles*

This card signifies the need to begin taking excellent care of something you haven't paid enough attention to. Consider all your priorities that can no longer be overlooked. This will allow you to go ahead in areas such as employment, finances, or anything else that may no longer be available to you.

As an archetype, it represents someone who accepts full responsibility for their faults and acts without blaming others. They can confess when they were wrong, and they will never find an excuse to get out of a situation when they are at fault. Highly principled, they will do whatever it takes to put things right.

Reversed Meaning: *Consideration*

Roy de Denier reversed signifies a situation where you are placing your priorities in second place because you don't feel the need to pay attention or consider them essential. It can also denote the archetype of a person who lacks tact, never takes responsibilities seriously, and decides to place blame on others.

The Feather

The belted kingfisher's feather advises you to take things slow, one step at a time, without rushing into something just because you are desperate to see results, since the overall outcome will not suit you. Remember, take time to achieve perfection.

LES COUPES

The suit of *Coupes* represents the emotions, social connection, and the sentimental, romantic, and spiritual aspects of life. In conventional tarot, this is the suit of Cups or Chalices.

You must learn to drink the cup of life as it comes ... without stirring it up from the bottom. That's where the bitter dregs are!

—Agnes Sligh Turnbull

AS DE COVPE

Ace of Cups

Like the Roman goddess Venus, a calm, young mermaid emerges from the cup to discover who needs love and how people fall in love. The chalice with water in which she poses is similar to Venus's shell, and under the water is where she pulls what she requires. She will teach love to those who do not know how, and she will take love away from those who abuse it for personal advantage. She is adamant about mending every damaged heart that has been unfairly beaten and smashed by evil brutes. The dove's feather reminds everyone that love, like all great things, comes to those who wait patiently for it.

Upright Meaning: *Love*

As de Coupe signifies love. Whether it's from their favorite person or their beloved pet they cherish, everyone wants to experience love in their lives. This feeling may be conveyed in various ways and should never be disregarded when expressed, since it demonstrates how much one loves another. This feeling must also be shared so both parties can experience it. This card instructs you to learn to appreciate everything and everyone around you, including people and things you must accept, since they have a purpose. When you love and appreciate what surrounds you, it makes you more attuned to nature and what it has to offer.

Reversed Meaning: *Expression*

You are blocked from love, and you have yet to express how much you adore or appreciate someone in your life who values and holds you close to them. In turn, this can leave you feeling lonesome and empty. Don't let this continue, because this could spiral you down into a state of depression. If you are feeling constrained from loving, slowly learn to seek the things you used to love and reopen your heart once again. Over time, your heart will be full of love once more, and you will recognize how this benefits you.

The Feather

The dove's feather advises you to get in touch with your feelings. You have been paying too much attention to logic and not understanding why you are feeling the way you do. Take the time to know what you need and who or what can help you. Write down all the things that make you feel good and bad, along with the reasons why they make you feel those ways. This will connect you with your emotions, to help you better understand how you feel.

TWO OF CUPS - PARTNERSHIP

DEUX DE COVPE

Two of Cups

These two cups stand united and not too far from one another, as they usually travel in pairs. They bring lovers together when they need to quench their thirst and help them develop intimate moments. The flamingo's feather between them is responsible for making people fall in love and forming a relationship of any sort.

Upright Meaning: *Partnership*

When *Deux de Coupe* appears in your reading, it illustrates the dynamics of an interpersonal connection and dedication to someone you trust. It is a relationship that provides mutual benefit and assistance to both parties and doesn't have to be romantic — there are many types of platonic relationships that can exist, such as friendships, and business or creative partnerships. When you are in a relationship, accepting the other person and understanding their shortcomings helps you maintain the magic of that connection. This card can also remind you to build a sense of goodwill where you can accept everyone around you, not just your partner.

When you can identify a mutual interest between yourself and those around you, open up yourself to those you trust. In doing so, what you need from them will help you give them what they need.

Reversed Meaning: *Mistrust*

The trust you once had in someone has been broken due to influences or misunderstandings that could not be resolved in time. This has created awkward tension between you, and communication is no longer harmonious. To rebuild trust, you must first acknowledge whether you want to remain in contact with the person. If you do, you will have to lay out some reasonable ground rules and expectations. But don't put all your eggs in one basket.

The Feather

The flamingo's feather advises you to pay close attention to a bond that is forming between you and someone you care about. This person can be key to helping you find happiness and helping you overcome troubles that linger in your life. Don't be afraid to acknowledge them, and make them feel welcomed and special. When you acknowledge this person, you are opening to an everlasting friendship or love interest.

THREE OF CUPS - BIRTH

TROIS DE COVPE

Three of Cups

Two cups stand together. They rejoice over the new cup which has been born from each other's productivity and is now being taken care of. For now, they will tend to the cup so it can prosper and be able to hold the liquids being poured into it. The swallow's feather will help to oversee the cup's progress.

Upright Meaning: *Birth*

Trois de Coupe describes the birth of a child or something that's been in development within you, such as a creative project or idea. Whatever it is, it will offer a considerable quantity of delight you can share with yourself or others. When it comes to a project, this will also provide a lot of pleasure. Regardless of whichever birth it may be, you are being asked to remain ready and say "no" to overstressing yourself. You are needed at your best mental and emotional state.

Reversed Meaning: *Scandals*

There are too many scandals circling you. You have no part in any of these, and slowly they are luring you in. You should start gathering information about where they are coming from and start informing people that you have nothing to do with them. Doing so may clear the air and keep your reputation safe.

The Feather

The swallow's feather advises you to form a bond with those in your circle who play a significant role. It is through these people that you will find the support you need to help you overcome the difficulties you are facing. When you get close to these people, you will form everlasting companions who will be there for you. To go about this, simply be yourself and show you are trustworthy.

QUATRE DE COVPE

Four of Cups

Four cups stand on each corner of the frame, where they embody the personification of a family in a household. Each mug protects each corner in order to avoid any unwanted intrusions which can disrupt their peace. The kiwi's feather ties everyone together and reminds them that family is and must be a priority to take care of.

Upright Meaning: *Family*

Quatre de Coupe represents your family and their wellbeing. The card reminds you to support everyone in your family to live happily and healthily. If you happen to be estranged from your family, do whatever you can to rebuild a solid connection. Ensure there is frequent communication so that you understand each other and prevent miscommunication that might lead to distress. Family are not only your 'blood relatives' but those with whom you have built an everlasting and trusting relationship. They are the people you should hold close. In being close to your family, you have allies to help you when you find yourself in hardship that is difficult to manage alone.

Reversed Meaning: *Disconnected*

Recently, you have become apathetic and disconnected from all the things you used to enjoy and people you loved being surrounded by. This card is asking you to reevaluate where you find yourself by understanding what got you into this mess in the first place. Keep attempting to do the hobbies you liked and hang out with the people you enjoy. This may reignite that spark you once had.

The Feather

The kiwi's feather advises you not to ignore gifts or affection given to you, since this comes from the bottom of people's hearts who genuinely love and care about you. Learn to accept what is being delivered and appreciate their efforts. When you receive the affections of others, you are letting yourself be accepted and understanding what makes you unique, and you, too, will learn how to show affection.

FIVE OF CUPS - CONNECTIONS

CINQ DE COVPE

Five of Cups

Five cups do their best to form a unique connection with one another in order to get the job done, and to oversee any problems which may bring them disruptions. Despite that they are an odd number, they are willing to oversee this minor issue, so they won't have to rely on an additional cup to even them out. For now, the eastern meadowlark's feather that accompanies them serves as a temporary replacement.

Upright Meaning: *Connections*

Drawing *Cinq de Coupe* indicates there are resources available to you from people more experienced than you in a particular field. This doesn't mean you aren't able to achieve what you want. To accept this help, you need a guide who can help you progress forward with your projects. People from all walks of life have something important and valuable to share with you. Dismissing them outright will not be a favorable action on your behalf. Build and establish relationships to become successful. When you do so, you will have much more success than had you tried to do it all yourself.

Reversed Meaning: *Blocks*

You find yourself too preoccupied with irrelevant things in your life, which, in turn, has left you blocked from learning to communicate or connect with others on a higher level. In order to overcome this blockage, you will need to learn to detach yourself from these irrelevant things that take up your time. This will help you to become less dependent.

The Feather

The eastern meadowlark's feather advises that you are at a point where you are losing hope. It is not in your best interest to do so, since hope is what you need to get through your problems and suffering. Retaining hope will help you explore solutions and answers to your problems, such as learning not to give up and look straight ahead when all seems to be falling apart.

SIX DE COVPE

Six of Cups

Six cups are gathered, grounded, and centered, and they know they must continue to develop their support for each other, despite all odds. Now they feel a sense of security, and they will see to it, and it continues to be this way. The pink-necked green pigeon's feather in the center serves as a purpose to give them the motivation that is needed.

Upright Meaning: *Continuity*

Six de Coupe indicates that anything started must be continued until it achieves its purpose and must not be stalled. If what you're working on seems terrific and secure, there's no need to stop. If there is a risk you don't feel prepared to take, walking away is not the best option. Putting it on hold and resuming it later when you feel the risk is not as high, or is more manageable, is the best approach. This card may also indicate that repetition is required to achieve the best outcome, or so you can study and polish your talents to prevent mistakes and disappointments. Simply keep doing what you're doing and wait for the results.

Reversed Meaning: *Disinterest*

Things you once got enjoyment from have now become tedious and dull, and you've lost the inspiration to pursue them. Disinterest only grows and makes you feel bad. It's time to take a break from it all and focus on something new that catches your attention. Novelty helps keep your attention focused and the waters of inspiration flowing. Embracing it can revitalize you, and your creativity. Then, you can return to those things you enjoyed, if it feels appropriate to do so.

The Feather

The pink-necked green pigeon's feather advises you that now is the time for you to feel blessed for what you have around you, since it has been bestowed upon you for a purpose. Although it's not much, it is much more than many people have, and for this you are lucky.

SEPT DE COVPE

Seven of Cups

Before becoming acquainted, these seven cups once stood on their own, not depending on anything to get them through their mission. Now that they realize they have so much in common, they have decided to unite and become one in order to see each other through any tasks at hand. The desert finch's feather inside the bottom cup reminds them to stand independently if needed.

Upright Meaning: *Individuality*

Sept de Coupe indicates this is a time for you to accomplish things independently without relying on anybody for assistance, even if it may sometimes appear harsh. This will give you a better and deeper insight into what you are skilled at and what needs improvement. More often than not, you should start pursuing your purpose and becoming a leader for yourself, rather than following in the footsteps of others. This may help you become much more self-sufficient, which, in turn, will result in not depending on anybody to do things the way you want to.

Reversed Meaning: *Rekindle*

There appear to be some issues with wanting to rekindle a relationship of some sort— romantic, friendship, etc.—with someone you deeply care for. There are obstacles getting in the way of this, such as personal problems. Before approaching someone, see to it that your problems are sorted out.

The Feather

The desert finch's feather advises you to keep an eye open for all the wonderful opportunities which are at your disposal, and understand that each brings a unique outcome when selected. Be very careful which one you choose and see to it that it can benefit you greatly.

HUIT DE COVPE

Eight of Cups

Here are eight cups that are involved with each other in order to help one another through any problems they are facing. They know very well that they also need to give each other much-needed space to sort their affairs into order. The mountain quail's feather in between the two cups reminds them to remain together.

EIGHT OF CUPS - INVOLVEMENT

Upright Meaning: *Involvement*

Huit de Coupe indicates that it is time to become deeply immersed in any pursuits that bring relaxation and fulfillment. Being involved in your community displays your dedication to people around you, which might open doors for you as you demonstrate the potential to achieve great things in life. This might also indicate becoming more connected with someone in your life with whom you have a lot in common — this could be a romantic or platonic attraction. The more involved you become, the more opportunities open up for you, and, in turn, you will also be more open to different perspectives that can influence you positively.

Reversed Meaning: *Effect*

Outside influences are starting to negatively influence your relationships, putting a wedge between communication and achieving goals. Spend more time looking at where these problems are coming from and attempting to fix them. You may need to implement some personal boundaries, such as saying "no" to demands on your time and energy, or perhaps you need to refrain from sharing too much of yourself with others, before it is too late.

The Feather

The mountain quail's feather advises you to stop taking on other people's demands. They are only wearing you out to the point where you could find yourself in the middle of a nervous breakdown. This abuse needs to stop, and only you can end it. Make a list of what you are not fond of and your expectations. When you do this, not only will you learn about yourself, but you will also learn from other people in the way they react to this.

NINE OF CUPS - HARMONY

NEUF DE COVPE

Nine of Cups

Despite being an odd number of cups, they are arranged in three rows of three cups each, creating a symmetrical and harmonious form. Everything around them is now protected, and they can be at peace and harmonious, content with each other's company. The scarlet tanager's feather resting horizontally at the bottom of the three cups substitutes itself as the tenth object.

Upright Meaning: *Harmony*

Personal troubles take their toll on you, weighing heavily on your shoulders and causing you setbacks. *Neuf de Coupe* guides you to begin working in harmony and peace to avoid this. When surrounded by negative individuals who bring difficulties into your personal space—either at work or elsewhere—do everything you can to avoid being engulfed in their troubles, since negativity is contagious. Find people who are empowering and radiate positivity, which you can apply in your life. Do this for yourself; don't ever doubt that you are entitled to live in peace. If and when you can, help others find harmony when their troubles take over.

Reversed Meaning: *Confusion*

Social situations often bring too much confusion, especially when someone does not know where they belong or what role to play. When faced with this type of problem, it will often become difficult for you to fit in, leaving you wondering where you truly belong. If you have given it your all and still feel you don't fit in, look for people who you can relate to and feel comfortable with. You'll be glad you did this, as you will have found a harmonious group that accepts you for who you are.

The Feather

The scarlet tanager's feather advises you to go out and make all your wishes come true, since you have earned this opportunity that you have waited so long for. Be sure your wishes are realistic and can help you in any way possible. When you have realistic wishes, this will lead you to be more grounded and down-to-earth.

TEN OF CUPS - LEADERSHIP

DIX DE COVPE

Ten of Cups

The group has now become crowded with so many cups that there is no more room for an additional one. The giant cup at the top has taken the role of the leader, and the rest of the mugs must obey its orders and commands to remain united. The lesser nighthawk's feather acts as a support for all of them to engage and work together.

Upright Meaning: *Leadership*

Dix de Coupe says it's time for you to take the wheels of leadership and be an exemplar for those around you to learn the value of honesty and courtesy. When you have good traits that serve a fantastic role in any relationship, individuals who know you hold you to high standards. Always learn to accept responsibility for your actions and never expect others to perform your work for you, since it is your mission, not theirs, and vice versa. Never forget to establish high standards, but not so high that they appear inauthentic and unattainable. When you establish high standards, you will paint a clear picture of what you will and will not tolerate. This will help you gain the respect from people around you.

Reversed Meaning: *Ungrateful*

You frequently forget to be grateful for those around you who have helped you. Without thanking them, it leaves a bad taste in their mouths. It may not be your intention, but this leads them to see you as ungrateful. In turn, nothing will work in your favor. The best solution to this is to say, "thank you" and return the favor when the occasion presents itself. This will leave people with a great impression of your appreciation and humility and will endear you to them.

The Feather

The lesser nighthawk's feather advises you to move away from any hardships. It encourages you to make your home a peaceful haven where you and anyone else who enters can feel at ease without feeling troubled and worried about things that serve no purpose. A place like this will bring good spirit and happiness for a long time.

PAGE OF CUPS - SHYNESS

VALET DE COVPE

Page of Cups

This dainty and sensitive young maiden stands isolated from her gossiping peers. She recalls past opportunities where she did what her heart desired, and contemplates past mistakes that led her to become withdrawn. She tried to become more adventurous, but she found she struggled to find the confidence to engage fully with the world. Hiding from the world hasn't necessarily worked for her either, minimizing her capacity to be social. Holding her razorbill's feather tightly, she realizes that she is not as timid as everyone thinks she is — she is simply being protective of her reputation and selective of whom she lets into her life.

Upright Meaning: *Shyness*

Sometimes, it may appear to others that you are aloof or detached. This isn't the case. Your genuine intentions are true, but you frequently have difficulties articulating what you believe. You struggle to demonstrate how you truly feel because you are sensitive and concerned about how others may interpret it. You don't want to stomp on anyone's toes. *Valet de Coupe* encourages you to express yourself authentically and let the rest flow. People will appreciate seeing the real, caring person you are.

As an archetype, this card represents someone who knows how to express how they feel but decides to keep their opinions to themselves because they fear being misunderstood. One way or another, they will find a way to let it be known to anyone interested. Please pay close attention to them, as they have much to say to you.

Reversed Meaning: *Misperception*

A situation has arisen where terrible feelings have accumulated toward someone, making it somewhat challenging to see any positivity toward them. Don't let these feelings cloud your perception. Try seeing things from a different perspective. Think of three things that are wonderful about them and notice how that begins to change your feelings toward them.

In reverse, this card represents someone who puts on pretenses to get what they can for their own benefit, without regard for others. While they're not being authentic, don't underestimate them — you can learn a lot from them, so long as you can see past the façade.

The Feather

The razorbill's feather advises you to start learning how to keep your friends by making them feel like they matter. It's time to weed out the ones who are not there for you, and start paying close attention to those who show you they care for you unconditionally. Giving your time and energy to those who care for you will leave you feeling loved and part of the community.

KNIGHT OF CUPS · OPENNESS

CAVALIER DE COVPE

Knight of Cups

This vibrant and charming young sea entity has ascended from the depths of the ocean, where he dwells happily with loved ones. His mission is to help everyone understand how to open their hearts and minds to endless possibilities, like the ones at the bottom of the ocean. The chalice he holds in his hands is filled with beautiful sensations one can enjoy if they are open to what life has to offer — only those willing to drop their excessive guard can truly enjoy it. The Cuban trogon's feather he holds in his hands is his reminder to never close himself off, no matter how difficult life becomes or if others refuse to open up.

Upright Meaning: *Openness*

You need to be open to the boundless and advantageous opportunities presented to you by individuals within your immediate circle and life in general. *Cavalier de Coupe* emerges from the ocean as a sign that you should confide in someone you trust. When you can show them you can be trusted, a good friendship will blossom.

As an archetype, this card depicts someone slowly attempting to open up, but unsure how to catch your attention. Listen and pick up on the subtle signs that the person is providing you. It may also represent a person who is listening to you open up. Nonetheless, open your heart and hear them out — you could learn a thing or two from them.

Reversed Meaning: *Accommodation*

A situation has arisen where you are not expressing what is felt to accommodate other people's liking. In turn, this leaves you feeling disappointed. Disregard what others think or say about you and express yourself authentically and respectfully.

As an archetype, this card reversed represents someone who is shut off from the world around them because of the many deceptions they have faced. Getting them to open up will take some time, so do not force or push them. The best thing you can do for them is offer your help and support on their terms. They will eventually learn to trust and open up to you.

The Feather

The Cuban trogon's feather advises you to be more sensitive about other people's mishaps and offer a lending hand or an ear to hear them out. Show them that they can share how they feel without feeling scared. But your sensitivity can only be stretched so far. Ensure you are not giving away too much of yourself. If you feel you are, keep away from those who are taking advantage of your generosity of spirit. Set your boundaries and let them work out how to help themselves. Open yourself just enough to show people you care, but also draw the line that you will not be taken for granted.

QUEEN OF CUPS - GUARDIANSHIP

REYNE DE COVPE

Queen of Cups

She sits passively watching everyone's motions and conversations, but she's actually seeing deeper into their hearts and tuning in to their vibrations. As she connects with the sensations and emotions around her, she can identify who is hurting and needs emotional support, which she excels at delivering. The healing process begins with a simple word or gesture of compassion. Her loving servant provides her a cup with the cures. The American redstart feather she clutches reminds her that her mission is to care for everyone in her realm, especially the feeble and delicate who lack a voice to express their anguish and hurt.

Upright Meaning: *Guardianship*

In a situation, this card indicates the capacity to assume guardianship over the wellbeing of everything you cherish, whether material or human. You place much too much importance on your privacy and would go to any length to protect it. You must realize that being alone is not always the best approach, so you can use some company from those you trust and who make you feel good about yourself.

As an archetype, it represents someone who understands how to keep their emotions under control and prevent conflict. When they are ready they will convey how they genuinely feel without having to disparage anybody around them, so that everyone has a clear understanding.

Reversed Meaning: *Doubt*

The memory of terrible past experiences are haunting you, causing you to become defensive and detached from people. Don't let past trauma take away your caring heart. Learn to open your heart again and become the person you want to be around others.

The archetype represented by this card reversed is someone who doesn't take care of what they have—people or materials—and disregards them. These things no longer have any value or purpose in this person's life. If you happen to be neglected by this type of person, detach yourself from them and seek those you can turn to for support.

The Feather

The American redstart's feather advises you to be in tune with what you need. Don't ignore that voice when it is warning you that something is not suitable, as it can potentially save you from a mishap. Never forget to be synchronized with your intuition and heart when they tell you what is best for you. When you listen to your heart and your intuition, they can both provide answers which you may not expect but will guide you into making the right choice. This, in turn, will help you to understand your gut feeling, and never doubt what you are feeling, no matter how bizarre it seems.

KING OF CUPS - OPTIMISM

ROY DE COVPE

King of Cups

The king has grown tired of running his country and going out of his way to make everybody happy so that he can be held in high esteem. In his personal life, there is nothing more than echoes of a past happy marriage and a family who hardly exchange words. What brings his energy down is watching his kingdom lose all hope. He understands there is so much he can do. The kingfisher's feather he holds helps him to remain optimistic, hoping it can project onto people who look up to him.

Upright Meaning: *Optimism*

This card illustrates a situation where emotional maturity and a sense of non-attachment are required for understanding the opinions of others without becoming directly involved. It also suggests there may be a way to heal from any emotional trauma inflicted on you. A helpful tip to heal from an emotional trauma is to find people who have dealt with something similar to what you've experienced. You can learn so many wonderful tips that you can apply to yourself.

As an archetype, *Roy de Coupe* represents those who strive to persuade others to see the bright side of any situation. This optimism comes from the mastery of their emotional self. Even in the face of terrible circumstances where they have no power, they are able to maintain their emotional intelligence to face the challenges ahead. Consequently, people might learn an important lesson and become more grateful for what they have.

Reversed Meaning: *Negativity*

You have been surrounding yourself with negative people and toxic conditions for so long that it has rubbed off on you. Now you are carrying this negative energy, and it's making life unpleasant for yourself and others. It's time for you to cut back on all this. You would benefit from a spiritual cleansing to move all this pestering energy away from you. Look for more positively driven people to surround yourself with and model their behavior.

As an archetype, this card reversed represents someone who is too negative, always finding the flaws in others to make them feel better about their own inadequacies and appear more reputable. Should you come in contact with someone like this, keep them at a distance. You don't need their negativity in your life.

The Feather

The kingfisher's feather advises you to develop some tolerance to withstand challenging situations. At times, people you find difficult to deal with will serve the purpose of teaching you a lesson, such as what triggers you and how to cope with it. Once you develop resilience, you will see how effortless it is to move through hardships.

LES BASTONS

The suit of *Bastons* represents desires, passions, and energies that are outgoing, energetic, creative, and conflictive. In conventional tarot, this is the suit of Wands.

There is no magic wand that can resolve our problems. The solution rests with our work and discipline.

—Jose Eduardo dos Santos

ACE OF WANDS - PASSION

AS DE BASTON

Ace of Wands

A furious dragon has risen from the flames, one half wrapped around a staff, the other gripping it tightly to avoid falling. The dragon bites his tail with his razor-sharp teeth to remind him he is still alive. This dragon is a muse for discovering one's sexual delights, and acts as a guide for those challenged by their sexuality. Given his fiery nature, and the summer tanager's feather, he demonstrates the rush of heat felt when the fire of our passion is ignited. He may manifest himself, combust, and disappear, only to reappear at another time and location.

Upright Meaning: *Passion*

As de Baston represents your passions and what you enjoy. You want to go on new passionate adventures to discover what you're into, what draws your attention, and what motivates you, but you prefer to keep this secret. This is the moment to start honoring your uniqueness and recognizing what makes you happy, without worrying about what others think of you. Once you understand this, you can value, accept, and enjoy yourself for who you are in your own body.

Reversed Meaning: *Burnout*

You have become disinterested and disengaged with people in your circle. You used to have so much fun hanging out with them, but now you lack the motivation to spend time with them, even though you desperately want to. Your detachment is due to burnout. You are advised to seek assistance from professionals to help you rebuild your inner fire and reclaim your desires. Once you start to heal from this malaise, your passion and drive will return, and you will have the energy to socialize with your beloved ones once more.

The Feather

The summer tanager's feather advises you to allow things to come to term accordingly and refrain from acting out. This can break the flow of your spontaneous, creative impulses, and the outcome will not be favorable. Let things flow as they should, and your creativity will expand — but keep a careful eye on it and be wary of burnout.

TWO OF WANDS - UNCOVERING

DEUX DE BASTON

Two of Wands

Two wands lie on the floor, one resting on the other. They have teamed up to be able to uncover the secrets life has in store for whoever possesses them. Many things will be uncovered, but one will need to hold themselves together for what's in store. The bittern's feather unites the two wands, making only two roads that can't be taken together.

Upright Meaning: *Uncovering*

Deux de Baston signifies that you are well on your way to discover new and exciting things, such as a new job or friendship, maybe even the answer to your problem. Keep in mind that you may not uncover the things you want such as large sums of money, but you will find what you need — things that are important to improve your life. Remember to show gratitude when you find these things, because this is a great privilege which not everyone enjoys.

Reversed Meaning: *Absence*

You've lost all your motivation to follow your aspirations. This lack of motivation is going to linger for a while. The best option for you is to get yourself up and follow what you have been anticipating. When you feel like giving up, remember that the goal you're close to reaching lies just ahead.

The Feather

The bittern's feather advises you to be bold in whatever you do and say. Never shy away from what you need to express or want to do, since no one else will do it for you. Be assertive and fulfill whatever needs to be done. When you are assertive, you are showing sheer confidence and proving that nothing can bring you down.

TROIS DE BASTON

Three of Wands

Three wands adorned with plants are bound together — but not by force, just by choice since it's the way they function. They are three, and each represents a path — a way to go for those who collect them. They represent the beginning, middle, and end. The long-tailed tyrant flycatcher's feather nestled between them is trying to find its way out.

Upright Meaning: *Focus*

Trois de Baston signifies that after a brief or extended time of reluctance, you are forging ahead in the direction you need to go without being pushed around. You are meant to be on this path, it is one you were meant to take. No matter what comes your way, you're not going back. You may either pursue one path to achieve all you desire, or you can choose multiple paths — so long as they serve to put past traumas behind you. Whichever direction you choose, you are so close to accomplishing your goal that it will be worth all the sacrifices you've had to make.

Reversed Meaning: *Self-discipline*

You know very well that you must carry on with responsibilities all by yourself. Still, instead, you depend on people to push you to do them. In turn, they are becoming exhausted and aggravated at your lack of self-discipline. It's time to exercise some self-discipline and not depend too much on others to do things for you. You can ask for assistance, but showing you are self-sufficient will open many doors for you.

The Feather

The long-tailed tyrant flycatcher's feather advises that you require direction to follow the path you are meant to be on, since you've been walking astray. This path will eventually lead you where you need to be; don't hesitate to get on it.

QUATRE DE BASTON

Four of Wands

Four wands are lying on the floor. They are unable to move or find something that can help them do what they must. Despite that, there are two on each side which have taken a break from doing what they must. They will realize that they must get back to finishing what they've set out to do. The partridge's feather resting between the two groups will be glad to give them a boost to regain energy to move.

Upright Meaning: *Retreat*

You've been doing too much, and it's time to sit back and relax momentarily. *Quatre de Baston* signifies the need for a little break to allow things to run their course. You may take this little pause or installment to observe how things are progressing and what is around you that you can use to thrive. However, just because you're pausing it doesn't mean that everything will be ruined or that everything will stay the same. On the contrary, you'll be able to witness how everything evolves on its own.

Only you can determine when it's time to return to doing what you did before.

Reversed Meaning: *Hesitation*

You have taken a break from your important projects. Rather than getting back to doing what you're meant to do, you're hesitating to return to fulfilling your responsibilities. Eventually, you will have to prepare yourself to come out of that shell you're in and start to work on your projects. Take solace in the knowledge that your break has been restorative, and this sense of hesitation is normal. You will see how quickly time flies by, and you will be getting better at finishing what you've started.

The Feather

The partridge's feather advises you to find a way to get out of a toxic relationship or workplace. You have tried everything in your power to do so but have been unsuccessful. If you can't find a way out, start looking for alternative plans which can help.

FIVE OF WANDS - OVERCOMING

CINQ DE BASTON

Five of Wands

Despite the hindrance endured earlier, an additional wand has joined the group of four, providing them with the ability to overcome that setback and many more. This fifth wand is a bit more powerful, and with the purple sunbird's feather on top, it charges it to exceed in doing more.

Upright Meaning: *Overcoming*

Cinq de Baston indicates overcoming impediments before you. Now that you've overcome whatever was standing in your way, you may concentrate on your top priorities before they go unfulfilled and unacknowledged. You now know how to move around obstructions if they reappear. Learn from this and use it as a model of how to overcome anything that prevents you achieving your goals. You will always have the upper hand and be able to overcome anything without being knocked back.

Reversed Meaning: *Indiscretion*

You're not being careful with what you say to others, and you are expressing your opinion when and where it's not welcomed. It's advisable to keep quiet and not cross any lines, to avoid facing backlash. First, ask if you can give your opinion about something or someone, and if you are welcomed to do so, do so with well-measured words.

The Feather

The purple sunbird's feather advises you that you will need to find a solution to meet the high demands that are asked of you. There is no escaping these demands, and you must deal with them accordingly, finding the time and space to sort them out. In doing so, you will be showing determination, good fellowship, and reliability.

SIX DE BASTON

Six of Wands

These six wands have distinctive energies, which they don't share too often unless they work together. When they work together, they remain in harmony. They will emanate the power needed to carry out important tasks. This harmony is provided by the golden eagle's feather, which lies in between the two groups of six.

Upright Meaning: *Collaboration*

It's time to let go of your pride and begin working with those who have more knowledge and skills than you in certain areas. Never consider yourself undervalued simply because you are working with others who have more expertise. Instead, see it as an opportunity to learn as much as possible. When partnering with another person, give it your all and study as much as possible. The more you know how to work with others, the stronger your bridges and connections will be any time you need assistance.

Reversed Meaning: *Lethargy*

You are not putting all your efforts into complying with any type of teamwork as you had agreed, and everyone around you is becoming impatient. They perceive you as lazy and useless. If you don't want to separate from the group and work on your own, you best start making an effort to participate. Show your peers you have a lot to offer. This will result in people wanting to work with you, and you may be surprised at how much easier it is to achieve in a group than on your own.

The Feather

The golden eagle's feather advises you to take the liberty and accept all the claims and felicitations you receive for your accomplishments. You've come a long way, and the least you can do is take time to enjoy what you have rightfully achieved.

SEVEN OF WANDS - STRUGGLE

SEPT DE BASTON

Seven of Wands

All seven wands have one mission: to get along and learn from one another as much as possible. They are having difficulty getting along with one another, which is driving a wedge between them. The glossy ibis' feather will do its best to ease the hardship.

Upright Meaning: *Struggle*

Sept de Baston signifies that you are struggling at present. Not due to any of your actions, but those of someone else. You must act quickly and plan how to get out of these situations before they escalate and leave you vulnerable. If you know the person putting you through this, you should approach them about it and take action before it's too late. Do your best to confront and resolve these challenges by learning to solve the more complex ones, and save the easy ones for last. But, most importantly, do not allow them to interfere with any area of your life. When you resolve these struggles, you will find the energy you need to be creative and reach your goals.

Reversed Meaning: *Attentiveness*

Chances are, your struggles are related to the attention you're paying to a situation. Because you were unable to find a way to improve things, you let the situation become bigger and more problematic than it already was. Discern between what you are responsible for, and what originates from beyond your control. You only need to attend to what you have power over. When you deal with things accordingly, it gives you more space to take a break, breathe, and prioritize what's most important.

The Feather

The glossy ibis' feather advises you to stand up for what you believe in, even if the rest of the world does not agree with you. Be considerate of other people's opinions, but don't let them affect you in any way.

EIGHT OF WANDS · SELF-REGULATION

HUIT DE BASTON

Eight of Wands

All these wands stand together in an unbreakable group. They stand like this to demonstrate how to remain indestructible. There are rules and protocols that must be obeyed to stay the way they are. The pallas' leaf warbler's feather, which is between them, helps them pay attention to things that can interfere and break them apart.

Upright Meaning: *Self-regulation*

Huit de Baston indicates the need to take control by keeping everything in order, even if it requires self-discipline. This can go a long way as it will help you to remain intact and have all your affairs in order. You are more likely to achieve anything you set out to do if you can always self-regulate. To avoid complications, always remember to govern yourself over issues, solutions, and anything else in your life. When you deal with your issues in a timely manner, you're training yourself to deal with future issues that may be complex.

Reversed Meaning: *Commitment*

Taking on short-term responsibilities will lead to more success than long-term ones. Sure, the bigger responsibilities may be much more beneficial for you over time, but the long-term route can be exhausting. Only dive into long-term responsibilities if you can handle the pressure. Deal with the short-term ones to get a sense of what's expected from you. When you do so, you learn to manage your energy better.

The Feather

The pallas' leaf warbler's feather advises you to start heeding all messages and communication coming your way, even if they seem irrelevant since they can all help you out of a fix. Work on how you can communicate efficiently as well.

NEUF DE BASTON

Nine of Wands

A new member is joining the group of eight wands, and this member has too much to learn about power and force. But before anything settles appropriately, there is an unwanted intrusion that will cause a disruption, bringing all plans to the ground. The blackbird's feather will help to keep the intrusion at bay.

Upright Meaning: *Disruption*

Neuf de Baston signifies that individuals and situations will disrupt your peace and everything you are currently working on. If these disruptions become too much for you to tolerate, you will need to learn how to deal with them or put an end to them. How far will your patience go? What is the utmost level of disruption you can tolerate? However, if you are rugged and robust, these factors will not be able to disrupt you or anything you are attempting to complete.

Reversed Meaning: *Setbacks*

You are facing too many difficulties without asking for help or assistance with overcoming them. This is a hindrance and prolonging anything you want to do in your life. Let your guard down, put your pride aside, and seek the help you need. In turn, you'll be glad you did because you won't have to deal with it alone.

The Feather

The blackbird's feather advises you that even though you are expecting the worst news possible, know and understand that it's not the end of the world. There are still lessons and solutions to ease the blowup that this will leave behind.

DIX DE BASTON

Ten of Wands

These ten wands are light as a feather, but heavy as stones. They represent what is needed to remain loyal to oneself, to others, and to goals and dreams waiting to be accomplished. The hoatzin's feather resting horizontally binds the wands to remain faithful to one another.

Upright Meaning: *Loyalty*

Dix de Baston indicates your loyalty is an essential part of working with others or when someone reveals confidential information to you. This loyalty is vital to maintaining trust in these relationships and you may risk breaking it if you take it for granted. If you do, remember that it will reflect negatively on you. Remember also to stay faithful to yourself and maintain your boundaries and commitments to your wellbeing. When you demonstrate loyalty to individuals around you, they will be loyal to you, resulting in far stronger connections in your life.

Reversed Meaning: *Disloyalty*

You're being disloyal and failing to keep your promises to others. Perhaps you aren't doing this intentionally. If so, now is the time to change your behavior before you are found out. If you don't rectify this, you will be confronted about it. By being disloyal and selfish, you are making yourself seem closed off and frugal and setting yourself up for failure. Learn to be honest and giving. When you do this, many possibilities will appear.

The Feather

The hoatzin's feather advises you to seek help to put an end to or to slow down your struggles. Keeping it all to yourself may lead to these difficulties multiplying and becoming overwhelming. Don't give up — know where to find the help you need when you feel it's too much.

PAGE OF WANDS - CREATIVITY

VALET DE BASTON

Page of Wands

This enticing young man stands in his garden, knowing he must continue with his creation but wondering what else it may need. The staff he's holding is his muse — a tool he carries with him to motivate and spark the fires of creativity. The shield in his hand is only part of the tool used to complete his masterpiece, but more is needed before it's finished. For now, with cassin's auklet's feather, he will jot down his ideas and gain inspiration so that once he has finished working on it, his project will be successful.

Upright Meaning: *Creativity*

A situation has emerged where you must refine your talents to improve and express what is in your thoughts. Start by investing time into something you enjoy doing, such as an artform. Never underestimate yourself or be ashamed of your artistic expression. It's yours, and you have the right to it.

As an archetype, *Valet de Baston* represents someone who is exceptionally creative and visually artistic. They can imagine and realize a wide range of ideas using several artistic methods. They get their ideas from every source they can find and will go to any extent to make them a reality.

Reversed Meaning: *Dimness*

You are confusing your desires with your needs, and not carefully selecting what you want for yourself. Drawing this card reversed suggests that you need to start seeking what is important to you and how it could benefit your whole health — mind, body, and emotions.

The reversed version of this archetype is someone who has no objectives or desires. They give into promiscuity and temptation, risking their—and others'—health and reputation. You may want to refuse this person's advances and persuasions to avoid mixing with the wrong crowd.

The Feather

The cassin's auklet's feather advises you to be more enthusiastic when you meet new people because that can give them the impression that you are wholehearted and accept people for who and what they are. Being passionate about what you do goes a very long way.

KNIGHT OF WANDS - URGES

CAVALLIER DE BASTON

Knight of Wands

This impatient and enraged centaur has decided that now is the time to wage war on the rivals, harassing and slaughtering his people. They were formerly renowned as peaceful creatures who preferred harmony over rioting and enjoyed settling problems by mutual agreements and friendliness, but those days are long gone. He lifts his horn to summon his commanders, urging them to prepare to go into battle. The staff in his hand represents his authority over his warriors. The blue grosbeak's feather he grips tells him that he did not want things to turn out this way. He was forced by circumstance.

Upright Meaning: *Urges*

You have too many desires to be met, but you must carefully choose the most important ones. This is not the moment to do something in vain or indulge curiosity, since it may get you in hot water. *Cavallier de Baston* asks you to eliminate what's not important and keep what is. This will help you meet your desires and make the process a smooth one.

As an archetype, this card represents someone who gives in to safe inclinations to explore their curiosity. This has positive outcomes for their health, finances, employment, and anything that needs to be taken care of quickly. You can learn much from them if you are ever needing some sound advice on how to take care of matters expediently.

Reversed Meaning: *Restraint*

You are not paying attention to your mind and body and are overworking them too much. It's time to slow down and heal yourself by learning to relax. When you are feeling restless or stressed out, find a quiet spot where you can meditate and get in touch with your higher self. This will help you become more aware of your mind and its contents.

As an archetype, this card reversed represents someone who is easily addicted to many unhealthy habits and substances. They are careless around other people. Don't follow their example. Learn to get away from unhealthy habits by enforcing healthy ones that can benefit your wellbeing.

The Feather

The blue grosbeak's feather advises you to be more adventurous. Seek out new places to visit or things you'd like to try, since they can get you out of your comfort zone. Without this sense of adventure, your life may seem a bit uninteresting.

QUEEN OF WANDS - PERSONALITY

REYNE DE BASTON

Queen of Wands

An elegant and regal queen sits on her throne, overhearing the loud, crass, and unflattering criticisms and laughter the women in her court are exchanging. She's bothered and offended by these women who are not composing themselves as madams and are carelessly dragging their reputations through the dirt. She knows she'll have to talk to them. As for her, she has nothing to hide and worry about since she understands herself, and her worth is represented by the staff she holds. With the roseate spoonbill's feather and her clothing, she sets a good example for those around her.

Upright Meaning: *Personality*

Reyne de Baston describes a situation where your personality must shine through. It is time for you to demonstrate who you are and what you represent. Be yourself without feeling ashamed. Some won't accept you, but many will.

As an archetype, this card represents someone with such a pleasant disposition that they attract many new acquaintances. People find it easy to get along with them. This individual not only attracts the attention of others, but also has the greatest of luck for taking leaps of faith.

Reversed Meaning: *Dishonesty*

This card reversed signifies a situation where you are not speaking truthfully, following the bad examples of others, and using intimidation to get what you want. All this will catch up to you if you don't change. Start by being sincere and understanding. When you do this, you will find that what you want to happen will do so more and more often.

As an archetype, the reversed version of this card represents someone who likes to intimidate people just to let others know that they are in charge and it's "their way or the highway". Do not give in to this person's intimidation. Instead, address their wrongdoings and learn from their example without following it.

The Feather

The roseate spoonbill's feather advises you to start demonstrating self-confidence in everything you do to lift your spirits whenever you feel down and need to give up. Never forget to show others that they, too, can be confident if they only try to do so. Being self-confident will help build (or rebuild) your self-esteem and is something others will learn from you.

KING OF WANDS - ATTITUDE

ROY DE BASTON

King of Wands

A handsome king sits on his throne, resting from a long journey. He is making drastic changes in his kingdom, and everything is going as expected. Growing annoyed by other monarchs' shortcomings and being questioned about his integrity, he showed a side of himself rarely seen and took everyone by surprise. Reflecting on that day, he feels a tad disappointed at having taken that drastic approach, causing him to bow in shame. Yet, he knows he was right to act out. The black-and-white warbler's feather in his possession reflects that deep down inside he enjoyed unleashing his hidden side and, if he had to, he would do it all over again without hesitation or guilt.

Upright Meaning: *Attitude*

This is when you must be an adult and think maturely to set an example for everyone else to follow. This will assist you in gaining the respect of others around you. When you stand up for yourself and set an example for others, you will show people you are true to yourself.

When you stand up for yourself, use facts when the other person is in the wrong. This can help you get your points across without having people second-guess what you are trying to say.

As an archetype, *Roy de Baston* represents someone who is mature and sets an example for anybody learning how to improve their professional abilities. Because of their integrity, honesty, and good reputation, everyone looks up to this person and considers them a role model. If you are in need of sound advice, seek this person out and maybe have them as a mentor so you, too, can learn as much as possible.

Reversed Meaning: *Exaggeration*

The reversed meaning of this card signifies a situation where you are blowing things out of proportion to gain attention. The current issues can be solved easily with patience and tranquility. No other help is required — don't turn away from them. Instead, go back, and fix them.

Roy de Baston reversed represents someone who likes to make a big deal of things, making people feel guilty about their responsibilities. There is no need to listen to someone like this. Know that they are wrong, and you have nothing to feel guilty about. When you ignore them, their exaggerations won't influence you, and you'll be able to achieve your outcomes without any stress.

The Feather

The black-and-white warbler's feather advises you to be a source of inspiration for someone who is going through difficult times. They may suffer from low self-esteem issues. This may serve as inspiration for you to be more kind to others and yourself.

LES ÉPÉES

The suit of *Épées* represents
the intellect, rationality,
the verbal, decisive, and
aggressive actions.
In conventional tarot,
this is the suit of Swords.

*Bombs and pistols do not make a
revolution. The sword of revolution is
sharpened on the whetting stone of ideas.*

—Bhagat Singh

ACE OF SWORDS - MENTALITY

AS D'ÉPÉE

Ace of Swords

This mighty griffin represents the human mind and its functions of thinking, solving problems, tapping into the unconscious mind, and seeing dreams and imagination at play. This winged creature holds on to the sword, representing the effects thoughts can have on the people around us and the consequences of acting out. He is the sensation when an idea rattles inside our head, like a bird locked in a cage trying to find a way out. The beast on top of the griffin biting the ostrich feather denotes how one can shape their thoughts and how even one's thoughts can work against them. The sword bending itself into a circle represents that our thoughts are infinite.

Upright Meaning: *Mentality*

As d'Épée signifies the time to begin thinking clearly and put all your wonderful and interesting ideas into motion. You want to do so much, but don't know where to start. Begin by writing down all your ideas and how they can benefit you and your plans. Reflect carefully on how you'd like to make your ideas a reality, without becoming confused with self-doubt. Take excellent care of your mind because it is the tool that allows you to create countless things. Start picking up active hobbies that you are interested in. To maintain a healthy mental state, focus on the good and avoid obsessing over situations that you have no control over. You'll find that when you have mental clarity, you will be able to think through situations far more effectively, which will impact decision-making and thus help you live your best life. You may also help someone to clear their mind when you notice they feel confused, since you have already experienced this.

Reversed Meaning: *Restlessness*

You are feeling restless and relentless to the point where your outlook on life and people is becoming negative. This mindset is clouding your thoughts, and you find yourself dwelling on past pains only to feel sorry for yourself. This is not making you feel any better. It's time for you to put all that to rest, get yourself up, and find something exciting that can keep your mind occupied. This, in turn, will have a dynamic change on your point of view of life.

The Feather

The ostrich's feather advises you that this is the time to become just and fair to everyone, including yourself. If you see any injustice, do whatever you can to make it right again, even if it means having to own up to your own mistakes.

DEUX D'ÉPÉE

Two of Swords

Two swords are together—as one—but different from each other, since they are used to perform various tasks. They are a yin-yang pair. They can't be used at the same time, but know they belong together as one. The shrike's feather in between lets them know they can't cross the line, must remain where they belong, and have to do their respective duties.

Upright Meaning: *Boundaries*

Deux d'Épée indicates it's time to begin limiting who can and cannot enter your circle of trust and personal space. You frequently feel the urge to welcome everyone into your life, oblivious to the fact that they can easily take advantage of your good nature. This is why you must establish limits and clarify what you do and do not accept from someone you are getting to know. Set boundaries not only for others, but also set them for yourself in terms of what you can and cannot do, what you are proficient in, and what requires practice. When you set boundaries, this will let people know what you will and will not tolerate, which, in turn, will bring you respect.

Reversed Meaning: *Limitations*

You're behaving as if you have no limitations, simply doing whatever you feel like without drawing the line where you need to stop. This is getting you into a great deal of trouble, and things are getting out of control. This behavior is also impacting others. Now is the time to know when and where to draw the line. Think of your wellbeing, and don't be afraid to cast out those who bring nothing but hardship. Doing this will help you keep yourself out of trouble. When you know your limitations, you're also not wasting energy on unnecessary things — energy that could be put to better use.

The Feather

The shrike's feather advises you to stop and analyze the obstacles and problems you are facing by not doing what you need to and ignoring your priorities. This will soon become a habit you won't be able to break away from.

THREE OF SWORDS · VICTORY

TROIS D'ÉPÉE

Three of Swords

For so many years, the two swords used to aid fighters in endless conflicts have grown old and unusable. Although their sharpness has worn out, reminders and memories of many victors who won have not gone away. The third sword in the middle is just as good as the other two, but newer and sharper. The torn, yellow-crowned night heron's feather is proof of that.

Upright Meaning: *Victory*

Trois d'Épée signifies triumph is within your grip, and a lot of success is following you little by little. It won't be long until it all piles up in front of you. You've climbed to the top and you're now carrying the torch of victory, despite any setback. This will not conclude here, as there are more opportunities for you to accomplish great success in your life. Remember to be an inspiration to people who can follow in your footsteps and become victors as well.

Reversed Meaning: *Annoyance*

Lately, you have seen that you have become unsuccessful, and it is causing you a great deal of frustration. You are moments away from giving up on yourself because you want success to be quick and easy. Since you know it's not, this is starting to bother you a lot. Your best course of action is to wait until success comes to you. If you are putting in the appropriate work, it will come in due course. If you can't wait, leave that dream somewhere safe and return to it at another time. The frustration will cloud your thoughts, so release that and get on with things.

The Feather

The yellow-crowned night heron's feather advises you that you are facing a time of loneliness. It's time that you went out and made some friends for the sake of having good company. Of course, you must choose wisely whom you will let in your circle of friends, since there are people who can take advantage of your generosity, and this will make you distrust people.

FOUR OF SWORDS · RESTRICTION

QUATRE D'ÉPÉE

Four of Swords

These four swords are ready to be used in the hands of those skilled in wielding them. The swords are selective of who will use them since they can cause such potential and irreversible damage. The goldcrest's feather in the center of the blades keeps those who are not skilled away.

Upright Meaning: *Restriction*

Quatre d'Épée suggests someone is taking advantage of you by stealing what you have. This is uncalled for, and you should not have to cope with it. You need to impose limitations and maintain your boundaries. This does not imply that you are becoming egotistical. Instead, it means taking care of the resources you still have. You may also impose restrictions and see how much you can withhold without breaking them. Respect and follow any limits placed on you and know when you may and may not cross the line. Doing so will teach you how to be tactful and how to compose and conduct yourself in a more sophisticated manner.

Reversed Meaning: *Impediment*

You have been feeling plenty of blockages that are not letting you think clearly. But you are ignoring these and refuse to get rid of them, knowing they are only hindering what you want to do. This is not favorable in any way. Ask for some help and find ways to liberate yourself from these blockages. Once you overcome those blockages, you'll see what's in store for you.

The Feather

The goldcrest's feather advises that it's time to gain a better perspective on the things you once sought out and all that you perceive to be negative. Your judgment has been clouded by too much negativity, and it's time to think clearly.

CINQ D'ÉPÉE

Five of Swords

FIVE OF SWORDS - BREAKTHROUGH

Four powerful swords have established themselves as a group — a union where it was only them and no other. With much potential and its distinct cutting edge, the fifth sword has made its breakthrough and added itself to the group. It is here to stay, holding the central position. Had it not been for the mockingbird's feather, this fifth sword would have been left wandering alone.

Upright Meaning: *Breakthrough*

Cinq d'Épée symbolizes that you have now crossed the finish line and have gained new information that you will put to use. You've worked too hard for too long to reach where you are and, despite the difficult road, you made it on your own. This is merely the beginning of your journey, and you will soon find yourself breaking into other areas that interest you. Now that you've made your breakthrough, it's time to become an expert in your field by being consistent in what you enjoy and love to do, no matter the sacrifice. It is time to show the world what you know and what you can do. Not only will you show everyone what you are capable of, but this will ignite and motivate you to do so much more.

Reversed Meaning: *Obstinate*

You have become too stubborn to go out and do something beneficial for yourself. You find it difficult to enter into any kind of reasoned discussion, and you refuse to listen to anyone with a valid point or acknowledge anyone who attempts to make you see where you may be wrong. It's time for you to swallow your pride and start paying attention to what you need to do to get yourself out of difficult situations. Doing so can make your life a little better and easier.

The Feather

You are gradually becoming careless and just thinking about yourself and what you need, which can leave you cold and hollow and potentially burn bridges you have made. The mockingbird's feather encourages you to be conscious and considerate of other people's needs. You'll find life more effortless when you include other people's needs as well as your own.

SIX OF SWORDS - ADAPTATION

SIX D'ÉPÉE

Six of Swords

A new sword has made its way into the group of five and will have to learn to adapt carefully to its purpose. Once it has done so, the six swords standing—three on each side—become accustomed to what they are used for. The oilbird's feather stabilizes all of them, helping them to adapt to any changes and outside influences.

Upright Meaning: *Adaptation*

Six d'Épée signifies the time to adjust to any new environment you have entered and start becoming acquainted with everything involved in it. This could be a new home, city, or workplace. It is challenging to learn to adapt to your new surroundings, such as fitting in or connecting with people you meet. Settling in will become easier once you begin practicing and learning from others around you. Adapting does not only refer to bodily changes but also to mental ones, such as learning to think and act differently. When you learn to adapt, everything will fall into place, and you will no longer have to worry about the adjustment.

Reversed Meaning: *Capitulation*

You have surrendered to your problems and vices too quickly without fighting, and now you are letting personal problems and influences take over. This has left you unable to speak and do anything for yourself. It's time to stand up to those who are bad influences on you and put an end to your problems. This will help set you free and you will have greater capacity to achieve your dreams.

The Feather

The oilbird's feather advises you to start looking for a place to go whenever things become too difficult at home. Take into account that this place does not have to be a physical location, it can also be a mental place where you can find peace and comfort. You deserve peace. When you find this peace and comfort, your physical and mental health will improve dramatically.

SEVEN OF SWORDS - SHARPNESS

SEPT D'ÉPÉE

Seven of Swords

There are seven swords, six of which at one point were sharp and resilient to anything and anyone, but not anymore. The new and seventh sword is much quicker and more dangerous if misused. The Atlantic puffin's feather by its side helps keep it from causing unwanted damage.

Upright Meaning: *Sharpness*

Sept d'Épée signifies the need to act quickly when you notice something wonderful and valuable — seize it before someone else does. Sharpness is related to how alert your brain is and how you observe things and realize whether something is out of place. It also refers to being able to focus your vision on one essential subject that you know needs immediate attention. When you do not put your intellect to use and lose interest in things, your capacity to remain keen might deteriorate. The best way to keep your intellect intact is to seek out solutions to problems you can solve by putting your mental energy into play, and you will see the wonders it can do for you.

Reversed Meaning: *Inconvenience*

You are becoming the type of person who only likes to see and think about what is convenient to you and what you can gain from it. This will only make you appear selfish and ignorant in the eyes of those in your circle. This will not help your cause, and you will have a bad reputation for being this way, leaving a bad taste in people's mouths. Don't be so rigid and let others share what's on their mind — you could learn a thing or two.

The Feather

The Atlantic puffin's feather advises you to start making it a regular habit to self-examine your faults and reflect on the actions for which you have been guilty. You often run away from them, and the only way to get rid of them is to face the music and accept the consequences. Accepting the consequences may seem daunting, but it will better prepare you to face the challenges life and the universe has in store for you.

EIGHT OF SWORDS - DEFENSE

HUIT D'ÉPÉE

Eight of Swords

There are eight swords, and they are divided into two groups — four on each side as a sign of equilibrium. These eight swords make sure that nothing goes wrong, and they are in charge of defending what is theirs and looking out for one another. Although not a sharp instrument, the fish crow's feather participates in supporting them in the process.

Upright Meaning: *Defense*

Huit d'Épée indicates the time to protect what is rightfully yours and to defend yourself whenever you feel taken advantage of. When you're with someone you care about and you get into an argument, avoid using physical or verbal violence — this will only make things much worse. This might result in a physical or verbal fight, leaving you hurt or in serious trouble — neither of which you can afford. Consider how you will defend what is yours, how you will go about it, and what resources you will employ if necessary. You can defend what is right verbally by speaking your mind with facts, as opposed to violence. When you do this your words can have a longer-lasting effect and may make others see your point of view.

Reversed Meaning: *Meddling*

Your curiosity has gotten the best of you, and now you are getting into other people's business when you know you are not being called to. This behavior is being noticed, and trouble is coming to you. Refrain from acting out on these impulses. Learn how to mind your own business by focusing on yourself. If your attention is always on others, you will miss very important signs about what is happening to you. When you keep your attention on the areas of your life that need it, you will be able to address things as they arise.

The Feather

The fish crow's feather advises you to stop avoiding responsibilities you know you must meet in order to get through the day. You dodge them sometimes, knowing they will eventually catch up to you. See to it that you oblige and follow them through.

NINE OF SWORDS · COURAGE

NEUF D'ÉPÉE

Nine of Swords

The eight swords on either side have been through and seen it all before, and nothing scares them. The new sword introduced into the group has a lot of work to do to become brave. The Carolina wren's feather standing by the sword in the center will give it the courage it needs when going into battle.

Upright Meaning: *Courage*

Neuf d'Épée signifies the necessity for you to have the confidence to confront challenges and the consequences of your actions. You understand that these difficulties will not go away on their own. You must take care of them before they get out of hand. This may be unexpected, and maybe even relentless, but there is no escape from it. When facing your fears, you get to know who you really are. When you can't face them alone, seek someone who can be there for you every step of the way. Once you've decided what to do, you can count on your bravery to face anything without fear.

Reversed Meaning: *Abandonment*

You are required to give your all to a project or a matter. You must show your dedication and efforts, but instead, you leave it half done and work on it whenever you feel like it and not pay any attention to it. Be mindful that you have made a promise to yourself that you will see it through until the end. Do not abandon this — there is a reason why you have been entrusted with this matter. Giving up on it means giving up on yourself. When you stick with it, you are showing others—and yourself—that you are trustworthy, and it will lead to better things in the future.

The Feather

The Carolina wren's feather advises you to find help for whatever is causing you difficulties. These are the kinds of problems that leave you unable to fulfill your goals and dreams. All this needs to come to an end as soon as possible. Find the assistance you need so that you can overcome these challenges. If you can beat these difficulties, you will have the strength to beat others.

DIX D'ÉPÉE

Ten of Swords

All ten of the swords have grown tired after being used too many times, not only for battles but other tasks. They are no longer as quick or as sharp as they used to be, and they no longer serve a purpose for anyone. The devil bird's feather in the center ignites the potential they need to return to how they once were.

Upright Meaning: *Exhaustion*

You are cramming so many chores into such a short amount of time that you cannot care for yourself or pay attention to your wellbeing. Your brain has gotten fatigued, muddled, and hazy, allowing you to become easily annoyed and lose your temper. *Dix d'Épée* indicates it is time to relax. Stop straining yourself so hard that you can't breathe or get back up. Pause to gather your thoughts and rest your mind and body so you may experience some comfort and tranquility. Learn to take a break every so often to avoid burning yourself out. When you do this, you will see you are preserving your vitality for greater things to come.

Reversed Meaning: *Frustration*

For whatever reason, you have lost a current position or an opportunity you have been aspiring to for a long time. Not only is it frustrating, but it is humiliating and a blow to your ego. Don't take your frustration out on anyone around you. Take a moment to engage in some self-reflection. Is there something you could have done better—or not at all—that would have prevented you from being in this situation? If you feel you can't come out of this on your own, ask for assistance and guidance from someone you trust. Listen to what they have to say, as they are removed enough from the situation to give you an objective outlook but close enough to you to care about what happens to you.

The Feather

You're going down a spiral and slowly sinking into your failures. You are now stuck and can't come out of this hole you've let yourself fall into. The devil bird's feather advises you that there's still the possibility for you to climb back up, slowly but surely. Once you do climb back up, you will see all the good things that were waiting for you to restore them.

PAGE OF SWORDS - PREPARATION

VALET D'ÉPÉE

Page of Swords

This young man is aware he's not a knight, but neither is he a child, and he is ready to take on any duty assigned to him. He had the most outstanding instructors and mentors who prepared him well to be an honest young man. He has learned to understand what he is doing and how to do it, and he is capable of taking on any work with success. The ribbon-tailed astrapia's feather in his hand reminds him that his teaching was difficult, and he had to fall and get back up countless times to maintain his ground, but he has no regrets. Once prepared, he waits carefully to see how he will accomplish his future objectives.

Upright Meaning: *Preparation*

Drawing *Valet d'Épée* suggests you are in a situation where you must start preparing yourself before trying to do something you're not comfortable with. By preparing, you are giving yourself room to carefully see if this is right for you. This will assist you in pulling back from it if it does not work out as you'd hoped.

As an archetype, this card represents someone who is constantly one step ahead of things and never jumps into anything without being thorough. This individual will tell others to do the same so that they may be safe and think before acting, to prevent making mistakes.

Reversed Meaning: *Misjudgment (of self)*

You have made a habit of underestimating yourself by bringing yourself down with harsh words and thoughts you inflict on yourself. Stop judging yourself so harshly. Give yourself credit for all the wonderful things you have done. You are worth it!

As an archetype, *Valet d'Épée* represents someone who likes to judge others poorly and make them feel unworthy. They are cruel and tactless and offer nothing encouraging to others out of spite.

The Feather

The ribbon-tailed astrapia's feather advises you to develop clear ideas and plans for whatever you are planning to do with your life or any projects you are working on. Failing to do this will result in epic failures, which you can't afford. Developing clarity and making appropriate plans means you will achieve the outcome you desire.

CAVALIER D'ÉPÉE

Knight of Swords

KNIGHT OF SWORDS - ENERGY

This centaur-like creature's vigor is enormous, and he can knock everyone in his path to the ground in a split second. Wielding his sharp sword, he can do and undo so much damage and good all at once, and nothing or no one can step in his way. If necessary, he can smash through cement and steel walls. He runs like lightning on the hard earth with the support of his powerful legs. The ruby-crowned kinglet's feather in his palm recharges him and gives him everything he needs to go forth and fight the wars he believes he will win.

Upright Meaning: *Energy*

This card signifies the capacity to draw energy from wherever you need to, and to use it to lift yourself up when you're down. Nothing can stop you with the power you have in your hands, and you will be able to march and accomplish everything you set your mind to.

As an archetype, *Cavalier d'Épée* describes someone who is constantly on the move and never takes a rest. In their opinion, life is too short to waste. When they accomplish something, it motivates them to search for new things to do and put their mind to use.

Reversed Meaning: *Persuasion*

This card reversed signifies that you are building a habit of forcing people to see things from your point of view just to feel that you're correct. This will only alienate you and leave you feeling lonely. Do you want to be right, or do you want to be effective? If you want to persuade people that your ideas are good, show your way of thinking in more inviting ways, and don't be harsh if they choose not to agree with you.

As an archetype, *Cavalier d'Épée* reversed represents someone who is too egocentric and often thinks they are twice as bright and better than anyone else. Essentially, they have narcissistic tendencies and look down on the less fortunate.

The Feather

What you see may not very well be what you think it is. The truth will hurt more due to the letdown. The ruby-crowned kinglet's feather advise you to use logic

before engaging in and undertaking a project or any type of commitment. Your ability to reason will help you see through the fog of illusion and help you make appropriate decisions that lead to good and fruitful outcomes.

QUEEN OF SWORDS - POSITION

REYNE D'ÉPÉE

Queen of Swords

The queen sits on her throne with a blank expression, so no one knows how she feels. Because many people can't recognize her in the role of leading her kingdom without her husband, the stress of attempting to adapt to other people's norms has taken a toll on her. Despite being obliged to perform many activities and present a public face that is not her own, she understands her place and position. The calandra lark's feather, which she carefully examines, serves as a reminder to never forget where she stands and to never allow anyone to force her away from the position she has battled so hard to be in.

Upright Meaning: *Position*

Reyne d'Épée suggests that you should begin to consider your existing situation. Whether it's your profession or any relationships, evaluate where you stand and whether you are appreciated sufficiently. If you do not have a place or a say, it may be time to consider quitting and getting on with your life. When you are somewhere you don't belong, you will feel like you are going nowhere. Find where you belong, even if it's somewhere you are not familiar with. You will start to feel full of life again, and it will feel like good things happen to you without any effort.

As an archetype, this card represents someone fully aware of where they are in life and where they are going. If they sense they no longer belong, they will not attempt to repair things and will look for another place to live.

Reversed Meaning: *Defensiveness*

This card in reverse signifies being defensive about what is being said to you, even if it's for your own good. This leads to you lashing out at others. Learn to calm down and listen to what is being said and ask for clarification if needed. Everything will make sense once you do, and chances are there was nothing to be concerned about.

As an archetype, *Reyne d'Épée* represents someone who never bothers to understand serious matters and makes up assumptions about things and people without facts. They are quick to jump to conclusions and make irrational decisions.

The Feather

The calandra lark's feather advises you to be direct in getting what you want, without having to beat around the bush. Be honest and upfront when you feel something is not going according to plan or if you have any doubts or concerns.

KING OF SWORDS - DETERMINATION

ROY D'ÉPÉE

King of Swords

This king is gallant, yet powerful and accelerated. Everyone who knows him knows not to cross him or get in his way. Even when he was preparing to be a rightful ruler of his country, he was trained to follow his internal instincts without listening to what others had to say. All those who work under him are expected to follow his example. Currently, he's expected to make a treaty with other countries, and as much as his group attempts to convince him otherwise, his mind is set and there is no turning back. The albatross feather he grips firmly in his hand inspires him to never ignore his determination.

Upright Meaning: *Determination*

This card signifies breaking free from the past and focusing on the present and future. If you want to live your life with the potential to overcome incapacities and achieve goals, this is how to get started. Begin by accepting that some things don't serve your highest purpose. Weed out what doesn't have any benefit in your life, and make space for that which will lead you to achieve your purpose in life. Remain determined to reach your goals, no matter what might get in your way.

As an archetype, *Roy d'Épée* represents someone who does not take "no" for an answer and is always willing to go the extra mile to achieve what they are passionate about. They have boundless energy, and may help anyone who needs a burst of drive and encouragement to feel less powerless. They can motivate even the most downtrodden of people.

Reversed Meaning: *Attachment*

When this card is drawn reversed, it suggests that you are attached to people and things that once held value to you. It is time to realize that you can no longer remain attached to them, and understand that it's time to let go. Whatever they were contributing to your life is no longer relevant. The attachment is draining for you both. By letting go, you are giving yourself— and them—a new lease on life, creating the space for something new to come along that serves you better moving forward.

As an archetype, *Roy d'Épée* reversed represents a person who is attached to the idea that things will be the same while knowing that is impossible. They are unable to change or accept that change happens.

Their conservative nature stifles their growth and development, and they are unable to let go of the past.

The Feather

The albatross' feather advises you to be more concise and articulate when speaking. To be understood and avoid miscommunications, you need to be clear and succinct. This will help you in the long run to get your point across and to be heard.

ABOUT THE ARTIST

Cuban-based artist **Alejandro R. Rozán's** work mainly revolves around the arcane mysticism of the tarot universe. Alejandro employs a variety of different techniques, including the combination of watercolors along with gouache, pencil, pen drawing, and digital drawing, among which his imitation of stained-glass art stands out the most.

Currently, Alejandro is working on a few tarot decks as both the illustrator and concept co-creator. Follow Alejandro on Instagram and Facebook to see updates and more information about his work.

- facebook.com/AlejandroRRozán
- instagram.com/alejandrorodriguezrozan

ABOUT THE AUTHOR

Jay R. Rivera is a Spanish-American author empath, medium, and tarot reader who lives in Texas, USA. His first break came after his award-winning and best-selling debut publication, *Beautiful Creatures Tarot*, which garnered him international acclaim.

Jay R. graduated from the University of Texas Rio Grande Valley with a Bachelor of Arts in Communication Studies. He majored in interpersonal and intercultural communications and minored in French and Spanish language studies, specializing in language translations. He spent a significant amount of time after receiving his degree as a language translator and instructor.

In his spare time, Jay R. enjoys studying and learning new languages and cultures, writing short fiction stories, reading and watching horror books and movies, performing shadow work tarot/oracle readings for people, volunteering and advocating for animal welfare and women's and LGBTQI+ rights. Most importantly, he enjoys spending time with his three pets: Lucky, Candy, and Molly.

Nothing makes him happier than meeting, learning from, and becoming acquainted with like-minded individuals from all walks of life. His goals as an author are for his works to reach a wide range of people and provide them with peace and comfort.

You can learn more about Jay R. and keep up with his future projects on his social media accounts and his website.

- jayrrivera.weebly.com
- facebook.com/jayrrivera151
- instagram.com/jayrrivera151
- twitter.com/jayrrivera151

More from Blue Angel Publishing®

MEDICINE HEART ORACLE
Shamanic Wisdom of the Divine Feminine

Alana Fairchild
Artwork by Sophie Wilkins

Connect with the eternal essence of Mother Earth to honour the natural wisdom and loving intelligence of your Medicine Heart. Within the soul-nurturing space of this sacred oracle, you will discover precious offerings nestled in seen and unseen dimensions. Breathe into your questioning and allow shamanic treasures from around the globe to reveal ancient pathways, creative visions and potent spirituality.

44 cards + 368-page full-colour guidebook set
Packaged in a hardcover box
ISBN: 978-1-922573-80-3

DREAMS OF GAIA TAROT
A Tarot for a New Era

Ravynne Phelan

This deck will strengthen your connection to your divine self, whilst helping you to identify and heal past experiences that hold you back from living to your fullest potential. *Dreams of Gaia Tarot* allows for a more personal, intimate, and effective system for using cards as a roadmap to navigate your life path. Embark on this extraordinary journey of undoing, of being, and becoming, and be inspired by the knowledge that all that manifests in your future is born of choices you make today.

81 cards + 308-page guidebook set
Gold-foil lettering on covers
Packaged in a hardcover box
ISBN: 978-1-922161-95-6

More from Blue Angel Publishing®

THE QUEEN MAB ORACLE
Divine Feminine Wisdom from the Queen of the Fae

Tess Whitehurst
**Artwork by Mélanie Delon
& Cecilia G.F.**

Ancient and powerful, Queen Mab is an elemental emissary of charm, moonlight and manifestation. Turn to her for meaning, revelation and insight into the poetry and empowerment at play within all that is and all you shall become.

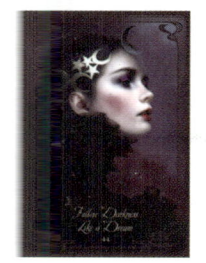

45 cards + 160-page full-colour guidebook set
Packaged in a hardcover box
ISBN: 978-1-922573-77-3

More from Blue Angel Publishing®

ORACLE OF THE SACRED HORSE

Kathy Pike
Artwork by Laurie Prindle

Ride higher planes of harmony and connection.

As well as offering honest and supportive responses to your questions, this oracle will deepen your kinship with the horse spirits so you can be enlivened by their freedom, grace, power, and agility — and feel these qualities reawaken in you, unbridled.

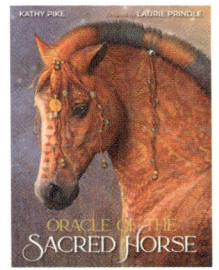

41 cards + 144-page full-color guidebook set
Gold-foil lettering on cover
Packaged in a hardcover box
ISBN: 978-1-922573-72-8

More from Blue Angel Publishing®

MAIDENS OF THE WHEEL ORACLE CARDS
Inner Journeys through the Cycles of the Year

Tammy Wampler

The Maidens of the Wheel have been known in many places and by many names throughout history. They dance through the cosmos, embodying inspiration and whispering guidance. They are here to empower and align you with sacred rhythms and lost traditions. Work with these elemental beings to discover harmony within the cycles of your life and embrace your true, unshakable center.

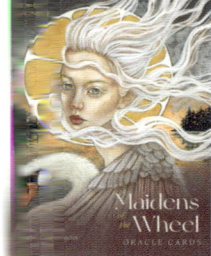

45 cards + 120-page full-color guidebook set
Packaged in a hardcover box
ISBN: 978-1-922573-90-2

More from Blue Angel Publishing®

THE PATH OF LIGHT ORACLE
Healing & Self-Mastery through the Wisdom of the Bhagavad Gita

Anthony Salerno
Artwork by Toni Carmine Salerno

Immerse yourself within a fusion of timeless teachings, spirited illuminations, transformative imagery, and loving intention to deepen your soul connections and discover wisdom, inspiration, and clarity. With in-depth messages and practical exercises inspired by the *Bhagavad Gita*, this enlightening oracle is invaluable for anyone seeking daily revelation or the joys of a more meaningful life.

39 cards + 160-page full-colour guidebook set
Packaged in a hardcover box
ISBN: 978-1-922573-82-7

NOTES

NOTES

NOTES

NOTES

BLUE ANGEL
PUBLISHING

For more information on this or
any Blue Angel Publishing® release
please visit our website at:

www.blueangelonline.com